Math Contests
for
High School
Volume 2

School Years: 1982-83 through 1990-91

Written by

Steven R. Conrad • Daniel Flegler

Published by MATH LEAGUE PRESS
Printed in the United States of America

Cover art by Bob DeRosa

Phil Frank Cartoons Copyright © 1993 by CMS

Second (Revised) Printing
Copyright © 1992, 1995
by Mathematics Leagues Inc.
All Rights Reserved

Math League Press
P.O. Box 720
Tenafly, NJ 07670-0720

ISBN 0-940805-04-9

Preface

Math Contests—High School, Volume 2 is the second volume in our series of problem books for high school students. The first volume contained the contests that were given during the 1977-78 through 1981-82 school years. (You may use the form on page 120 to order any of our 6 contest books.) The current volume contains the 54 contests given from 1982-83 through 1990-91.

These books gives classes, clubs, teams, and individuals diversified collections of high school math problems. All of these contests were used in regional interscholastic competition throughout the United States and Canada. Each contest was taken by about 80 000 students. In the contest section, each page contains a complete contest that can be worked during a 30-minute period. The convenient format makes this book easy to use in a class, a math club, or for just plain fun. In addition, detailed solutions for each contest also appear on a single page.

Every contest has questions from different areas of mathematics. The goal is to encourage interest in mathematics through solving *worthwhile* problems. Many students first develop an interest in mathematics through problem-solving activities such as these contests. On each contest, the last two questions are generally more difficult than the first four. The final question on each contest is intended to challenge the very best mathematics students. The problems require no knowledge beyond secondary school mathematics. No knowledge of calculus is required to solve any of these problems. From two to four questions on each contest are accessible to students with only a knowledge of elementary algebra.

This book is divided into four sections for ease of use by both students and teachers. The first section of the book contains the contests. Each contest contains six questions that can be worked in a 30-minute period. The second section of the book contains detailed solutions to all the contests. Often, several solutions are given for a problem. Where appropriate, notes about interesting aspects of a problem are mentioned on the solutions page. The third section of the book consists of a listing of the answers to each contest question. The last section of the book contains the difficulty rating percentages for each question. These percentages (based on actual student performance on these contests) determine the relative difficulty of each question.

You may prefer to consult the answer section rather than the solution section when first reviewing a contest. The authors believe that reworking a problem when the answer (but *not* the solution) is known often helps to better understand problem-solving techniques.

Revisions have been made to the wording of some problems for the sake of clarity and correctness. The authors welcome comments you may have about either the questions or the solutions. Though we believe there are no errors in this book, each of us agrees to blame the other should any errors be found!

Steven R. Conrad & Daniel Flegler, contest authors

Acknowledgments

For her continued patience and understanding, special thanks to Marina Conrad, whose only mathematical skill, an important one, is the ability to count the ways.

For her lifetime support and encouragement, special thanks to Mildred Flegler.

To Alan Feldman, who suggested several stylistic changes from the first volume to this one, we offer our thanks.

To Brian and Keith Conrad, who did an awesome proofreading job, thanks!

To Daniel Will-Harris, whose skill in graphic design is exceeded only by his skill in writing *really* funny computer books, thanks for help when we needed it most: the year we first began to typeset these contests on a computer.

Table Of Contents

School Year	Contest #	Page # for Problems	Page # for Solutions	Page # for Answers	Page # for Difficulty Ratings
1986-1987	1	26	82	115	117
1986-1987	2	27	83	115	117
1986-1987	3	28	84	115	117
1986-1987	4	29	85	115	117
1986-1987	5	30	86	115	117
1986-1987	6	31	87	115	117
1987-1988	1	32	88	115	118
1987-1988	2	33	89	115	118
1987-1988	3	34	90	115	118
1987-1988	4	35	91	115	118
1987-1988	5	36	92	115	118
1987-1988	6	37	93	115	118
1988-1989	1	38	94	116	118
1988-1989	2	39	95	116	118
1988-1989	3	40	96	116	118
1988-1989	4	41	97	116	118
1988-1989	5	42	98	116	118
1988-1989	6	43	99	116	118
1989-1990	1	44	100	116	118
1989-1990	2	45	101	116	118
1989-1990	3	46	102	116	118
1989-1990	4	47	103	116	118
1989-1990	5	48	104	116	118
1989-1990	6	49	105	116	118
1990-1991	1	50	106	116	118
1990-1991	2	51	107	116	118
1990-1991	3	52	108	116	118
1990-1991	4	53	109	116	118
1990-1991	5	54	110	116	118
1990-1991	6	55	111	116	118

The Contests

November, 1982 – April, 1991

HIGH SCHOOL MATHEMATICS CONTESTS

Math League Press, P.O. Box 720, Tenafly, New Jersey 07670-0720

Contest Number 1

November 2, 1982

Name _____ Grade Level _____ Score _____

Time Limit: 30 minutes

Answer Column

1-1.   What is the simplified value of $(121)^2 - (2)(121)(21) + (21)^2$?

1-1.

1-2.   In the diagram, the congruent circles are tangent to the larger square and each other as shown; and their centers are vertices of the smaller square. The area of the smaller square is 4. What is the area of the larger square?

1-2.

1-3.   Let $10^{101} - 1$ be written as an integer in standard form. What is the sum of the digits of this integer?

1-3.

1-4.   My accurate watch has only one hand, an hour hand. At the precise moment that this hand points directly to the 22-minute mark, what is the exact time? (Disregard A.M. or P.M.)

1-4.

1-5.   Two identical jars are filled with equal numbers of marbles. The marbles are colored red or white. The ratio of red to white marbles is 7:1 in Jar I and 9:1 in Jar II. If there are 90 white marbles all together, how many red marbles are in Jar II?

1-5.

1-6.   What are all ordered pairs of numbers (x,y) which satisfy
$$x^2 - xy + y^2 = 7 \text{ and } x - xy + y = -1?$$

1-6.

HIGH SCHOOL MATHEMATICS CONTESTS

Math League Press, P.O. Box 720, Tenafly, New Jersey 07670-0720

Contest Number 2   **December 7, 1982**

Name _____ Grade Level _____ Score _____

Time Limit: 30 minutes	*Answer Column*
2-1. Suppose $N^{1982} = 1982^{1982}$. If $N \neq 1982$, what is the real value of N?	2-1.
2-2. What is the *least* possible value of the sum $$\lvert x - 1 \rvert + \lvert x - 3 \rvert + \lvert x - 5 \rvert?$$	2-2.
2-3. The population of Sun Belt City increased by 25% in 1978, then by 20% in 1979—but it decreased by 20% in 1980, then by 25% in 1981. By what percent did the population of Sun Belt City decrease over this four-year period?	2-3.
2-4. If $\dfrac{1}{x^3} - \dfrac{1}{x^2} - \dfrac{1}{x} - 1 = 0$, what is the value of $x^3 + x^2 + x + 1$?	2-4.
2-5. The positive integer N has exactly eight different positive integral factors. Two of these factors are 15 and 21. What is the value of N?	2-5.
2-6. In the diagram (not drawn to scale), $\overline{CD}$ is a diameter of circle O. If arc ED is a 50° arc, and $m\angle EAD = 50$, what is $m\angle DAB$? [NOTE: All points which look collinear *are* collinear.]	2-6.

Solutions on Page 59 • Answers on Page 114

HIGH SCHOOL MATHEMATICS CONTESTS

Math League Press, P.O. Box 720, Tenafly, New Jersey 07670-0720

Contest Number 3

January 11, 1983

Name _____ Grade Level _____ Score _____

Time Limit: 30 minutes

Answer Column

3-1.   There is only one positive integer which is exactly twice the sum of its digits. What is this two-digit number?

3-1.

3-2.   What are both values of x which satisfy

$$x + \frac{1}{x} = 5 + \frac{1}{5}?$$

3-2.

3-3.   The value of $17x + 51y$ is 85. What is the value of $19x + 57y$?

3-3.

3-4.   Determine, in simplest form, the value of

$$\sin^2\left(\tfrac{\pi}{8}\right) + \cos^2\left(\tfrac{3\pi}{8}\right) + \sin^2\left(\tfrac{5\pi}{8}\right) + \cos^2\left(\tfrac{7\pi}{8}\right).$$

3-4.

3-5.   In the accompanying diagram, each circle has a radius of 1, and the circles are externally tangent as shown. What is the area of the shaded region?

3-5.

3-6.   What is the integer x which satisfies

$$10^x < \tfrac{1}{2} \times \tfrac{3}{4} \times \tfrac{5}{6} \times \tfrac{7}{8} \times \ldots \times \tfrac{99}{100} < 10^{x+1}?$$

3-6.

Solutions on Page 60 • Answers on Page 114

HIGH SCHOOL MATHEMATICS CONTESTS

Math League Press, P.O. Box 720, Tenafly, New Jersey 07670-0720

Contest Number 4   **February 8, 1983**

Name _____ Grade Level _____ Score _____

Time Limit: 30 minutes   *Answer Column*

4-1.	There are three different digits such that any two of them, written in any order, serve as the digits of a two-digit prime. What are all three of these digits?	4-1.
4-2.	Suppose $x = t^2 + t$ and $y = t^3 + t^2$. If $x = 2$, what are the two possible values of y?	4-2.
4-3.	A regular pentagon and a square share a common side, as shown at the right. What is the measure of $\angle ABC$?	4-3.
4-4.	Batman, Superman, and Wonder Woman compete in a series of daily 3-way races. For each race, the probability that Batman wins is $\frac{1}{6}$, the probability that Superman wins is $\frac{1}{2}$, and the probability that Wonder Woman wins is $\frac{1}{3}$. On a day that Batman doesn't win, what is the probability that Superman beats Wonder Woman?	4-4.
4-5.	If $f(2x) = x^2 + 4x + 1$, what are all values of t for which $f(\frac{t}{2}) = \frac{-11}{4}$, where f represents a function?	4-5.
4-6.	What is the perimeter of a regular dodecagon (a polygon which has 12 sides) whose area is $24 + 12\sqrt{3}$?	4-6.

Solutions on Page 61 • Answers on Page 114

5

HIGH SCHOOL MATHEMATICS CONTESTS

Math League Press, P.O. Box 720, Tenafly, New Jersey 07670-0720

Contest Number 5   **March 15, 1983**

Name _____ Grade Level _____ Score _____

Time Limit: 30 minutes   *Answer Column*

5-1. What is the value of x which satisfies $\sqrt{x} + \sqrt{x} = \sqrt{36}$?   5-1.

5-2. The infinite geometric sequence which begins
$$2^{300}, 2^{298}, 2^{296}, 2^{294}, \ldots$$
contains only one odd integer. This odd integer is the nth term of the sequence. What is the value of n?   5-2.

5-3. Let P denote the product of all the positive primes less than 100. What is the units' digit of P?   5-3.

5-4. In the diagram at the right, which is *not* drawn to scale, *ABCDE* is an inscribed pentagon and arc *DE* is a 70° arc. What is $m\angle A + m\angle C$?   5-4.

5-5. There are two real values of r for which
$$x^4 - x^3 - 18x^2 + 52x + k$$
has a factor of the form $x - r$. One of these values is $r = 2$. What is the other value of r?   5-5.

5-6. What is the exact numerical value of $\csc 20° - \cot 40°$?   5-6.

Solutions on Page 62 • Answers on Page 114

Contest Number 6   April 12, 1983

Name _____ Grade Level _____ Score _____

Time Limit: 30 minutes   *Answer Column*

6-1. What is the perimeter of the only rectangle whose diagonals each have a length of 10 and whose sides have integral lengths?

6-1.

6-2. Write, as a three-digit number, the final three digits of 5^{100}.

6-2.

6-3. What is the smallest value of d which satisfies
$$a^2 + b^2 + c^2 = d^2,$$
where a, b, c, and d are positive integers, not necessarily different?

6-3.

6-4. If $\dfrac{\log a}{\log b} = 1000$, what is the numerical value of $\dfrac{\log\left(\frac{a}{b}\right)}{\log b}$?

6-4.

6-5. If $\sqrt{4+x} + \sqrt{10-x} = 6$, what is the value of $\sqrt{(4+x)(10-x)}$?

6-5.

6-6. What is the value of k for which the system
$$r^2 + s^2 = t,$$
$$r + s + t = k$$
has exactly one solution (r, s, t)?

6-6.

HIGH SCHOOL MATHEMATICS CONTESTS

Math League Press, P.O. Box 720, Tenafly, New Jersey 07670-0720

Contest Number 1   **November 1, 1983**

Name _____ Grade Level _____ Score _____

Time Limit: 30 minutes   *Answer Column*

1-1. If the time right now is 9 A.M. (Standard Time), what time (Standard Time) will it be 23 999 999 hours from now? (Include an A.M. or a P.M. in your answer.)

1-1.

1-2. The ratio of the measures of two complementary angles is 4 to 5. The smaller measure is increased by 10%, By what percent must the larger be decreased so that the two angles remain complementary?

1-2.

1-3. What is the positive integer x for which $\sqrt{x}^{\sqrt{x}^{\sqrt{x}}} = 16$?

1-3.

1-4. A grid has 100 rows and 100 columns, numbered from 1 to 100 as shown in the diagram. In row 2, every second box is shaded. In row 3, every third box is shaded. From then on, every nth box of row n is shaded. Which is the only column to contain 5 (vertically) consecutive shaded boxes? [NOTE: Row 1 is left unshaded.]

1-4.

1-5. In a 5×12 rectangle, a diagonal is drawn and circles are inscribed in both of the right triangles formed. What is the distance between the centers of these circles?

1-5.

1-6. What are all ordered triples of numbers (x,y,z) which satisfy the system of equations
$$(x+y)(z+1) = 24,$$
$$(x+z)(y+1) = 24, \text{ and}$$
$$(y+z)(x+1) = 24?$$

1-6.

Contest Number 2   December 6, 1983

Name _____ Grade Level _____ Score _____

Time Limit: 30 minutes   *Answer Column*

2-1. August 8, 1964 (8/8/64) was a square root date because both the month and day are square roots of the last two digits of the year. How many square root dates will there be during the next century?
                                                                      2-1.

2-2. A cube is illustrated in

the diagram at the right.

In this cube, what is the

measure of $\angle ABC$?
                                                                      2-2.

2-3. Find all values of x which satisfy both $x^2 - 8 \le 2x$ and $x^2 - 2x \ge 8$.
                                                                      2-3.

2-4. Which is greater:

$$A = (1983)(1 + 2 + 3 + \ldots + n + \ldots + 1984), \text{ or}$$
$$B = (1984)(1 + 2 + 3 + \ldots + n + \ldots + 1983)?$$

Write "A" if A is greater, or write "B" if B is greater.
                                                                      2-4.

2-5. A median of triangle ABC divides it into two triangles of equal perimeter. The length of this median is 21 and the length of the side to which it is drawn is 56. What is the perimeter of $\triangle ABC$?
                                                                      2-5.

2-6. In an experiment, Jimmy the Greek draws cards, one at a time, from a well-shuffled (standard) 52-card deck until all 13 hearts have been drawn. On which (numbered) draw is he most likely to find the 13th heart?
                                                                      2-6.

HIGH SCHOOL MATHEMATICS CONTESTS

Math League Press, P.O. Box 720, Tenafly, New Jersey 07670-0720

Contest Number 3   **January 10, 1984**

Name _____ Grade Level _____ Score _____

Time Limit: 30 minutes   *Answer Column*

3-1. The sum of the squares of the lengths of all the sides of a rectangle is 100. What is the length of a diagonal of the rectangle?	3-1.
3-2. What are all three pairs of positive integers (a,b) which satisfy $$2^4 + a^b = 2^5?$$	3-2.
3-3. How many integral values of n satisfy the inequality $0 \le n^2 \le 100$?	3-3.
3-4. Heeding the advice to "Go West, young man," Harold and Horace Greedy set out for Las Vegas to make their fortunes. Luck was with the Greedy brothers, for each doubled his money every hour. Harold, who began with $20, gambled for 20 hours and then sent his fortune home. The next day, Horace began with $40 and gambled until his fortune matched his brother's. For how many hours did Horace Greedy gamble that day?	3-4.
3-5. The symbol $[x]$ represents the greatest integer which is less than or equal to x. What is the value of x for which the product of x and $[x]$ equals 28?	3-5.
3-6. What is the exact value of the only real root of the equation $$x^3 + 6x^2 + 12x + 24 = 0?$$	3-6.

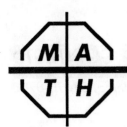

HIGH SCHOOL MATHEMATICS CONTESTS

Math League Press, P.O. Box 720, Tenafly, New Jersey 07670-0720

Contest Number 4

February 7, 1984

Name _____ Grade Level _____ Score _____

Time Limit: 30 minutes

		Answer Column

4-1. Let $N = 20 \times 30 \times 50 \times 70 \times 110 \times 130$. What is the smallest positive prime number which is *not* a factor of N?

4-1.

4-2. In (non-degenerate) isosceles triangle ABC, the perimeter is 40, and AB is twice AC. Find AB.

4-2.

4-3. Consider the line segment in the xy-plane whose left endpoint has coordinates $(-1,0)$ and whose right endpoint has coordinates $(3,0)$. Let this segment be divided into 1000 congruent segments, with points of division marked $P_1, P_2, \ldots, P_{999}$, going from left to right. What are the coordinates of P_{60}?

4-3.

4-4. What are all values of x which satisfy $x^2 - \cos x + 1 = 0$?

4-4.

4-5. If $\dfrac{x + yi}{1 + i} = \dfrac{7}{7 + i}$, where x and y are real, what is the value of $x+y$?

4-5.

4-6. If both a and b are positive integers, the equation $\sqrt{10} = \sqrt{a} + \sqrt{b}$ has no solutions. For how many positive integral values of $x \le 1000$ does

$$\sqrt{x} = \sqrt{a} + \sqrt{b}$$

have at least one solution in positive integers?

4-6.

Solutions on Page 67 • Answers on Page 114

11

Contest Number 5   March 13, 1984

Name _____ Grade Level _____ Score _____

Time Limit: 30 minutes   *Answer Column*

5-1. What is the smallest positive integer that leaves a remainder of 10 when divided into 90?

5-1.

5-2. Three of the vertices of the rectangle shown are the midpoints of three of the sides of $\triangle ABC$. If the area of $\triangle ABC$ is 24, what is the area of the rectangle?

5-2.

5-3. The lengths of the sides of a (non-degenerate) triangle are 3, 4 and x, where x is a positive integer. In a second such triangle, the lengths of the sides are 3^2, 4^2, and x^2. Find all possible values of x.

5-3.

5-4. Methuselah took a job that paid $20\,000$ the first day, $10\,000$ the second day and $5\,000$ the third day. Thereafter, the job paid half as much each day as the previous day. To the nearest dollar, how much money did Methuselah earn during the 900 years that he worked?

5-4.

5-5. If p and q are the roots of $2x^2 - 5x + 1 = 0$, what is the value of
$$\log_2 p + \log_2 q?$$

5-5.

5-6. What are all values of x between $0°$ and $360°$ which satisfy
$$(5 + 2\sqrt{6})^{\sin x} + (5 - 2\sqrt{6})^{\sin x} = 2\sqrt{3}?$$

5-6.

HIGH SCHOOL MATHEMATICS CONTESTS

Math League Press, P.O. Box 720, Tenafly, New Jersey 07670-0720

Contest Number 6   **April 10, 1984**

Name _____ Grade Level _____ Score _____

Time Limit: 30 minutes   *Answer Column*

6-1. For which value of x will $\frac{3+x}{4+x}$ and $\frac{6+x}{8+x}$ be equal? | 6-1.

6-2. What is the simplified value of $\frac{4444^4}{2222^4}$? | 6-2.

6-3. If $x^{100} = 2x^{50}$, what are both possible values of x^{200}? | 6-3.

6-4. What is the ordered pair of real numbers (x,y) for which | 6-4.
$$(x + y - 5)^2 + (x - y - 1)^2 = 0?$$

6-5. The lengths of the sides of convex quadrilateral $ABCD$ are 5, 6, 7, and x. If $\sin A = \sin B = \sin C = \sin D$, what are all possible values of x? | 6-5.

6-6. Triangle ABC, with obtuse angle B, is inscribed in a circle. Altitude $\overline{CH}$ of the triangle is tangent to the circle. If $AB = 6$ and $BH = 8$, what is the area of the circle? | 6-6.

Solutions on Page 69 • Answers on Page 114

Contest Number 1   October 30, 1984

Name _____ Grade Level _____ Score _____

Time Limit: 30 minutes   *Answer Column*

1-1.   What is the only integer between 1500 and 2500 which is an integral multiple of both 2^5 and 2^5-1?

1-1.

1-2.   As shown at the right, two congruent circles intersect so that the area of their common region is equal to the sum of the areas of their other two regions. If the area of their common region is 24π, what is the circumference of one of the circles?

1-2.

1-3.   What is the real value of x which satisfies

$$(2^{12} + 2^{-12})(2^{12} - 2^{-12}) \; = \; 8^x - 8^{-x}?$$

1-3.

1-4.   I have 1 brother and 2 sisters. My mother's parents have 10 grandchildren, while my father's parents have 11 grandchildren. If no divorces or re-marriages occurred, and if none of my father's brothers or sisters married any of my mother's sisters or brothers, how many first cousins do I have?

1-4.

1-5.   What are all positive integral values of n for which the expression $\dfrac{n^3 - 12}{n - 4}$ has an integral value?

1-5.

1-6.   Let r be a root of

$$x^4 - x^3 + x^2 - x + 1 = 0.$$

What is the value of

$$r^{40} - r^{30} + r^{20} - r^{10} + 1 = 0?$$

1-6.

HIGH SCHOOL MATHEMATICS CONTESTS

Math League Press, P.O. Box 720, Tenafly, New Jersey 07670-0720

Contest Number 2   **December 4, 1984**

Name _____ Grade Level _____ Score _____

Time Limit: 30 minutes   *Answer Column*

2-1.   What is the value of x which satisfies
$$\frac{17}{85} + \frac{19}{95} + \frac{21}{105} + \frac{23}{115} + \frac{25}{125} + \frac{x}{135} = 1?$$

2-1.

2-2.   What is the largest integral factor of $111\,111\,111\,111$ which is less than $111\,111\,111\,111$?

2-2.

2-3.   Each time the two hands of a certain standard 12–hour clock form a 180° angle, a bell chimes once. From noon today until noon tomorrow, how many chimes will be heard?

2-3.

2-4.   Harry the handy homeowner cleared a rectangular plot of land and covered it with gravel. Then he purchased 9 square wooden sections of side-lengths 2, 5, 7, 9, 16, 25, 28, 33, and 36. By placing the squares on the gravel with no two overlapping, Harry built a patio which exactly covered the graveled surface. What is the perimeter of Harry's new patio?

2-4.

2-5.   What are all ordered pairs of positive integers (x,y) which satisfy
$$xy + 6x - 11 = x^2?$$

2-5.

2-6.   What is the area of a trapezoid whose altitude has a length of 12 and one of whose perpendicular diagonals has a length of 15?

2-6.

Solutions on Page 71 • Answers on Page 114   15

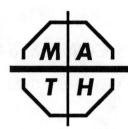

HIGH SCHOOL MATHEMATICS CONTESTS

Math League Press, P.O. Box 720, Tenafly, New Jersey 07670-0720

Contest Number 3   **January 8, 1985**

Name _____ Grade Level _____ Score _____

Time Limit: 30 minutes   *Answer Column*

3-1. What are all positive integers x for which $(x)(x) = x^x$?

3-1.

3-2. In simplest form, what is the numerical value of
$$(\sqrt{1985})(\sqrt[3]{1985})(\sqrt[6]{1985})?$$

3-2.

3-3. For every positive integral value of n, $n!$ represents the product of the first n positive integers. As an example, $6! = 6\times5\times4\times3\times2\times1 = 2^4\times3^2\times5$. What is the value of n for which
$$n! = 2^{25}\times3^{13}\times5^6\times7^4\times11^2\times13^2\times17\times19\times23?$$

3-3.

3-4. Two triangles share a common side. The lengths of the sides of the first triangle are in the ratio 5:6:7, while those of the second are in the ratio 4:9:11. If the lengths of all six sides are integral, what is the smallest possible length of this common side?

3-4.

3-5. One ordered triple (x,y,z) which satisfies the system
$$x - 2y + kz = 0,$$
$$2x - y + 3z = 0,$$
$$3x - 3y - 2z = 0$$
is $(0,0,0)$. What is the only numerical value of k for which this system has a solution other than $(0,0,0)$?

3-5.

3-6. A scientific supply house sells every integral gram weight from 1 gram to 100 grams inclusive. What is the least number of these weights a pharmacist would need to use, together with a two-pan balance scale, to measure correctly any integral gram-weight from 1 gram to 100 grams? [NOTE: Weights may be placed on either or both pans of the balance scale.]

3-6.

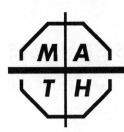

HIGH SCHOOL MATHEMATICS CONTESTS

Math League Press, P.O. Box 720, Tenafly, New Jersey 07670-0720

Contest Number 4   February 5, 1985

Name _____ Grade Level _____ Score _____

Time Limit: 30 minutes   *Answer Column*

4-1. If every side of a (non-degenerate) triangle has a different integral length, what is the smallest possible length of its shortest side?

4-1.

4-2. Of the following pairs (x,y), which is the *only* one that will *not* satisfy the equation $187x - 104y = 41$?

(107,192), (211,379), (314,565), (419,753), (523,940)

4-2.

4-3. Al and Barb both tried to solve the equation, $Ax^2 + Bx + C = 0$. However, each made exactly one error in copying the equation. The solutions of Al's equation were –2 and $-\frac{3}{2}$, but his value of A was wrong. The solutions of Barb's equation were 2 and 3, but her value of B was wrong. What are the solutions of the *correct* equation?

4-3.

4-4. The graphs of the three equations

$$y - |y| = 0,$$
$$x - 3 + |x - 3| = 0, \text{ and}$$
$$y - x + |y - x| = 0$$

are all drawn in the coordinate plane. How many ordered pairs of integers (x,y) satisfy all three equations?

4-4.

4-5. If a and b are one-digit positive integers, what are all fractions $\frac{a}{b}$ for which the infinite geometric series $\frac{a}{b} + \frac{a}{b^2} + \frac{a}{b^3} + \ldots$ has a sum of $\frac{1}{3}$?

4-5.

4-6. One solution of the equation $(x - a)(x - b)(x - c)(x - d) = 9$ is $x = 2$. If $a, b, c,$ and d are different integers, find the value of $a + b + c + d$.

4-6.

Solutions on Page 73 • Answers on Page 114

HIGH SCHOOL MATHEMATICS CONTESTS

Math League Press, P.O. Box 720, Tenafly, New Jersey 07670-0720

Contest Number 5   **March 12, 1985**

Name _____ Grade Level _____ Score _____

Time Limit: 30 minutes   *Answer Column*

5-1. Nineteen soldiers, numbered 1 through 19, stood in a circle in clockwise numerical order, all facing the center. They began to count out loud in clockwise order: the first soldier called out the number 1, the second called out 2; and each soldier then called out the number 1 more than the number called to his right. What was the number of the soldier who called out the number 1985?	5-1.
5-2. Let x be the smallest of three positive integers whose product is 720. What is the largest possible value of x?	5-2.
5-3. In simplest form, what is the numerical value of $$\frac{5^2 + 10^2 + 15^2 + \ldots + 90^2 + 95^2 + 100^2}{1^2 + 2^2 + 3^2 + \ldots + 18^2 + 19^2 + 20^2}?$$	5-3.
5-4. Simplify completely: $$\frac{1}{\sqrt{1} + \sqrt{3}} + \frac{1}{\sqrt{3} + \sqrt{5}} + \frac{1}{\sqrt{5} + \sqrt{7}} + \frac{1}{\sqrt{7} + \sqrt{9}}.$$	5-4.
5-5. If $0 \le x \le \pi$, find, in radians, all values of x which satisfy $$\log_{\frac{1}{2}}\sin^2 x + \log_{\frac{1}{2}}\cos^2 x = 3.$$	5-5.
5-6. The lengths of the three altitudes of a triangle are 12, 15, and 20. What is the area of the triangle?	5-6.

© 1985 by Mathematics Leagues Inc.

HIGH SCHOOL MATHEMATICS CONTESTS

Math League Press, P.O. Box 720, Tenafly, New Jersey 07670-0720

Contest Number 6   **April 16, 1985**

Name _____ Grade Level _____ Score _____

Time Limit: 30 minutes   *Answer Column*

6-1. What is the value of x for which

$$\sqrt{\frac{1}{9} + \frac{3}{9} + \frac{5}{9}} = \sqrt{\frac{1}{9}} + \sqrt{\frac{3}{9}} + \sqrt{\frac{x}{9}}?$$

6-1.

6-2. A rectangle and a square are inscribed in congruent circles. The rectangle has a width of 6 and a length of 8. What is the area of the square?

6-2.

6-3. What are all real values of x which satisfy

$$x^{1985} - x^{1983} = x^{1984} - x^{1982}?$$

6-3.

6-4. The square of 999 999 999 is an 18–digit number. How many of these 18 digits are 9's?

6-4.

6-5. During the summer of 1983, the McDonald's Corporation ran a promotional game. With each purchase, a customer received a game card. Each game card had 10 spaces hidden from view. In 8 of these spaces, the names of 8 different McDonald's products appeared. In a 9th space, 1 of these 8 product names appeared again. Thus, these 9 spaces contained only 1 possible pairing of product names. The remaining space contained something different; we'll call it an "X." To play, the game card spaces were unhidden, 1 at a time, in any order. Play ended when either the pair was uncovered (a "win" of that product) or the X appeared (a loss). Thus, every card could be a "winner." What was the probability of winning this game?

6-5.

6-6. Factor $1 + x + x^2 + x^3 + x^4 + x^5$ as far as is possible using only polynomials with integer coefficients.

6-6.

Solutions on Page 75 • Answers on Page 114

HIGH SCHOOL MATHEMATICS CONTESTS

Math League Press, P.O. Box 720, Tenafly, New Jersey 07670-0720

Contest Number 1   **October 29, 1985**

Name _____ Grade Level _____ Score _____

Time Limit: 30 minutes   *Answer Column*

1-1.	As shown, $\overline{AD}$ passes through centers A, B, C, and D of four congruent tangent circles. If $AD = 24$, what is the area of one of the four circles?	1-1.

1-2.	What are both values of x which satisfy $$2^2 + 4^2 + 6^2 + 8^2 = 1^2 + 3^2 + 5^2 + 7^2 + x^2?$$	1-2.

1-3.	What is the ordered pair of real numbers (x,y) for which $$x + y = 100 \quad \text{and} \quad x^2 - y^2 = 100?$$	1-3.

1-4.	If $a{\uparrow}b$ means a^b, what is the value of x which satisfies $$4{\uparrow}(3{\uparrow}2) \div (4{\uparrow}3){\uparrow}2 = 4{\uparrow}(3{\uparrow}x)?$$	1-4.

1-5.	Just prior to an early-season game, Slugger Smith had gotten a hit in (exactly) 30% of his "at bats," for a batting average of (exactly) .300. Because of that game, Smith's batting average fell to (exactly) .200. What is the fewest number of "at bats" that Slugger Smith could have had in that game?	1-5.

1-6.	Let N be the largest integer for which both N and $7N$ have exactly 100 digits each. What is the 50th digit (from the left) of N?	1-6.

HIGH SCHOOL MATHEMATICS CONTESTS

Math League Press, P.O. Box 720, Tenafly, New Jersey 07670-0720

Contest Number 2   **December 3, 1985**

Name _____ Grade Level _____ Score _____

Time Limit: 30 minutes | *Answer Column*

2-1.   For what value of k is the displayed factoring valid? | 2-1.

$$1985^2 + 1985^3 = (k)(1 + 1985)$$

2-2.   The sum of the squares of the lengths of the three sides of a right triangle is 200. What is the length of the hypotenuse? | 2-2.

2-3.   If a, b, and c are the smallest possible positive integers for which $3a = 4b = 5c$, what is the sum $a + b + c$? | 2-3.

2-4.   What is the difference between the smallest perfect square larger than 1 million and the largest perfect square smaller than 1 million? [Here, a *perfect square* has a square root which is an integer.] | 2-4.

2-5.   Each of the 4 cards shown at the right has a letter on one side and a digit on the other side. Now read the *test sentence* below: | 2-5.

$\boxed{A}$ $\boxed{F}$ $\boxed{2}$ $\boxed{3}$

> *Whenever there is a vowel on one side of a card, there is an even number on the other side of that card.*

Identify every card you *must* turn over to determine if the *test sentence* above is true or false for this set of 4 cards.

2-6.   Burgers are sold plain or with any selection of available condiments. Burgers with a different selection of condiments (including plain) are considered different types. If Burger Queen has 192 more types of burgers than Windy's, but only 2 more condiments than Windy's, how many types of burgers does Windy's have? | 2-6.

Solutions on Page 77 • Answers on Page 115   21

Contest Number 3   **December 17, 1985**

Name _____ Grade Level _____ Score _____

Time Limit: 30 minutes   *Answer Column*

3-1.   In terms of x, what is $x\%$ of $x\%$ of $x\%$ of $1\,000\,000$?   3-1.

3-2.   In a triangle containing an obtuse angle, the lengths of the sides, in increasing order, are the integers 3, 4, and x. What is the value of x?   3-2.

3-3.   What is the average value of all integers n for which   3-3.

$$400 < |n| < 800?$$

3-4.   In the diagram (which is *not* drawn to scale), each point of the inner square is 1 cm from the nearest point of the outer square. If the area of the region between the two squares is 20 cm^2, what is the area of the inner square, in cm^2?   3-4.

3-5.   Factor $4x^3 + 6x^2 + 4x + 1$ as far as possible using only polynomials with integer coefficients.   3-5.

3-6.   If a, b, c, and d are four *different* numbers for which   3-6.

$$a^4 + a^2 + ka + 64 = 0,$$
$$b^4 + b^2 + kb + 64 = 0,$$
$$c^4 + c^2 + kc + 64 = 0, \text{ and}$$
$$d^4 + d^2 + kd + 64 = 0,$$

what is the value of $a^2 + b^2 + c^2 + d^2$?

HIGH SCHOOL MATHEMATICS CONTESTS

Math League Press, P.O. Box 720, Tenafly, New Jersey 07670-0720

Contest Number 4

January 21, 1986

Name _____ Grade Level _____ Score _____

Time Limit: 30 minutes

	Answer Column
4-1. What is the positive value of x for which $$\sqrt{3^2 + 4^2 + 12^2} = \sqrt{3^2 + 4^2} + \sqrt{x^2}?$$	4-1.
4-2. What are both non-zero values of x for which $(x^x)^{1986} = 1$?	4-2.
4-3. If 1, 2, and 4 are three of the digits of the four-digit number N, and if N is divisible by 4, what is the greatest possible value of N?	4-3.
4-4. What is the probability that a point which is interior to a circle of radius 2 is further than 1 unit from the center?	4-4.
4-5. In the set of perpendicular segments shown at the right, $AB = 10$ and every other segment is 1 unit shorter than the previous one (so $BC = 9$, $CD = 8$, $DE = 7$, etc.). What is the (straight-line) distance from A to K?	4-5.
4-6. If $x^2 < 1000$ and $y^2 < 2000$, how many different ordered pairs of positive integers (x,y) have a sum divisible by 3?	4-6.

© 1986 by Mathematics Leagues Inc.

Solutions on Page 79 • Answers on Page 115

23

Contest Number 5   **March 4, 1986**

Name _____ Grade Level _____ Score _____

Time Limit: 30 minutes   *Answer Column*

5-1. A positive integer such as 4334 is a palindrome if it reads the same
      forwards or backwards. What is the only prime palindrome with an
      even number of digits?

      5-1.

5-2. The rectangle shown at the right has been
      divided into 12 congruent squares. If the
      length of a diagonal of one of the squares
      is 4, what is the length of a diagonal of the
      original rectangle?

      5-2.

5-3. There are eight numbers which can be written with four 2's and no
      other symbols. These eight numbers are:

$$2222, \; 222^2, \; 22^{22}, \; 2^{222}, \; 22^{2^2}, \; 2^{22^2}, \; 2^{2^{22}}, \text{ and } 2^{2^{2^2}}.$$

      Of these, which one represents the largest number?

      5-3.

5-4. What is the value of n which satisfies

$$\frac{1}{n} + \frac{2}{n} + \frac{3}{n} + \ldots + \frac{n-2}{n} + \frac{n-1}{n} = 1986?$$

      5-4.

5-5. In degrees, what are all ordered pairs of angles (x,y) for which
      $0° \le x \le 90°$, $0° \le y \le 90°$, and

$$\sin^2 x + \sin^2 y = \sin x + \sin y?$$

      5-5.

5-6. What is the smallest fraction that is a positive integral multiple of
      each of the fractions $\frac{6}{11}$, $\frac{5}{22}$, and $\frac{4}{33}$?

      5-6.

HIGH SCHOOL MATHEMATICS CONTESTS

Math League Press, P.O. Box 720, Tenafly, New Jersey 07670-0720

Contest Number 6   April 8, 1986

Name _____ Grade Level _____ Score _____

Time Limit: 30 minutes   *Answer Column*

6-1.   What is the only value of x for which $\dfrac{x^2 - 1}{x - 1} \neq x + 1$?   6-1.

6-2.   In a circle, chords $\overline{AB}$ and $\overline{CD}$ divide the circle into 4 congruent sectors. If $AB = 10$, what is AC?   6-2.

6-3.   What is the value of x which satisfies
$$2^8 + 2^8 + 2^8 + 2^8 + 2^8 + 2^8 + 2^8 + 2^8 = 2^x?$$
     6-3.

6-4.   When I am as old as Sue is now, Sue will be 4 years older than I am now. How much older is Sue than I?   6-4.

6-5.   In rectangle $ABCD$, AD is twice AB, N is the midpoint of $\overline{AD}$, and M is the midpoint of $\overline{BN}$. What is the value of $m\angle NMD + m\angle NBD$?   6-5.

6-6.   In *simplest form*, what is the rational number c which satisfies
$$\log_3 a + \log_{27} b = c,$$
$$ab^3 = 1986, \text{ and}$$
$$a^3 b = 9?$$
     6-6.

Solutions on Page 81 • Answers on Page 115

Contest Number 1   October 28, 1986

Name _____ Grade Level _____ Score _____

Time Limit: 30 minutes   *Answer Column*

1-1.   When all 8 positive integral factors of 30 are multiplied together, the product is 30^k. What is the value of k?

1-1.

1-2.   In square *ABCD*, drawn at the right, $EB = 3$ and $FC = 4$. If $\overline{AC}$ and $\overline{EF}$ bisect each other, what is the area of square *ABCD*?

1-2.

1-3.   Each root of $x^2 - 5x - 6 = 0$ is 1 more than a root of $x^2 + px + q = 0$. What is the value of p?

1-3.

1-4.   Smalltown has only two people who have the same (two-letter) initials. What is the largest population that Smalltown could possibly have?

1-4.

1-5.   Mr. Jordan painted a continuous, closed curve C on the gym floor. When he finished, he walked around on the gym floor, crossing the curve 1986 times in the act of leaving the gym. Of all possible curves C he could have drawn, what is the least number of times Mr. Jordan needed to cross his curve in order to leave the gym?

1-5.

1-6.   What are all ordered triples of integers (a,b,c) for which

$$ab + ac + bc = a + b + c + abc?$$

1-6.

Contest Number 2   December 2, 1986

Name _____ Grade Level _____ Score _____

Time Limit: 30 minutes   *Answer Column*

2-1. The sum of two positive numbers equals the sum of the reciprocals of the same two numbers. What is the product of these two numbers?

2-1.

2-2. What are the 4 integral values of x for which $|x^2 - 9|$ is a prime number?

2-2.

2-3. What is the remainder when 66^{1986} is divided by 12?

2-3.

2-4. Very few people are aware of the growth pattern of Jack's beanstalk. On the 1st day it grew to a height of 100 meters. Then, on the 2nd day, its height increased by $\frac{1}{2}$ (50%), on the 3rd day by $\frac{1}{3}$ ($33\frac{1}{3}$%), on the 4th day by $\frac{1}{4}$ (25%), and so on, so that on the nth day ($n \geq 2$) its height increased by $\frac{1}{n}$. How many days did it take to reach a height of 5000 meters?

2-4.

2-5. In the diagram shown at the right, $\overline{OA} \perp \overline{OC}$ and $\overline{OB} \perp \overline{OD}$. If $m\angle AOD = 4(m\angle BOC)$, what is $m\angle AOD$?

2-5.

2-6. If $x = \sqrt[3]{20 + 14\sqrt{2}} + \sqrt[3]{20 - 14\sqrt{2}}$, what is the numerical value of $x^3 - 6x$?

2-6.

Solutions on Page 83 • Answers on Page 115

HIGH SCHOOL MATHEMATICS CONTESTS

Math League Press, P.O. Box 720, Tenafly, New Jersey 07670-0720

Contest Number 3   **January 6, 1987**

Name _____ Grade Level _____ Score _____

Time Limit: 30 minutes   *Answer Column*

3-1. I bought a new car. Lee said it was a blue Dodge, Pat said it was a black Chevrolet, and Sandy said it was a black Ford. If each person correctly identified either the make of the car or its color, but not both, what was the color and the make of my new car?

3-1.

3-2. What are both values of x which satisfy $x^2 + 1986x = 1987$?

3-2.

3-3. The average of 10 numbers is 63. The average of 6 of these numbers is 57. What is the average of the other 4?

3-3.

3-4. What is the largest integral value of x for which
$$3^{x+2} < 3x + 2?$$

3-4.

3-5. In the diagram, the concentric circles have O as their common center. A radius of the smaller circle is 1 and a radius of the larger circle is 2. Both $\overline{AO}$ and $\overline{BD}$ are perpendicular to $\overline{OC}$. What is $m\angle BAO$?

3-5.

3-6. Simultaneously, 3 satellites began to orbit the earth at constant speeds. When the 1st completed x orbits, it had made 80 more orbits than the 2nd and 100 more than the 3rd. When the 2nd completed x orbits, it had made 25 more orbits than the 3rd. Find x.

3-6.

Contest Number 4   February 3, 1987

Name _____ Grade Level _____ Score _____

Time Limit: 30 minutes   *Answer Column*

4-1.   If $\left(\dfrac{2}{x} - \dfrac{x}{2}\right)^2 = 0$, what is the value of x^6?

4-1.

4-2.   What are both values of x for which $x\%$ of $x\%$ equals $x\%$?

4-2.

4-3.   In the diagram, M is the midpoint of the semicircular arc drawn on one side of a 6 by 7 rectangle. What is the perimeter of isosceles triangle MBC?

4-3.

4-4.   If i represents the imaginary unit, what is the value of
$$i^{1985} + i^{1986} + i^{1987} + i^{1988}?$$

4-4.

4-5.   What is the smallest positive integer N for which all the digits in the product $9N$ are 1's?

4-5.

4-6.   On the 30-question AHSME contest, an unanswered question is worth 2 points and a correct answer is worth 5 points. No points are given for an incorrect answer. A score of 100 or more *qualifies* a student for the next test. A student answering 14 questions needs all 14 correct to qualify—but a student who answers 15 questions can answer 1 incorrectly and still qualify! Thus, *qualification* requires the same minimum number correct (14) whether answering 14 or 15 questions. For some integers N, qualification requires the same minimum number correct whether answering N, $N+1$, or $N+2$ questions. What are all such values of N?

4-6.

Solutions on Page 85 • Answers on Page 115   29

Contest Number 5   March 3, 1987

Name _____ Grade Level _____ Score _____

Time Limit: 30 minutes   *Answer Column*

5-1. To express 10 as a sum of *different* powers of 2, we would write $10 = 2^3 + 2^1$. The sum of the exponents of these powers is $3 + 1$, or 4. If 100 were expressed as a sum of *different* powers of 2, what would be the sum of the exponents of these powers?

5-1.

5-2. In terms of percent, which fits better—a round peg in a square hole or a square peg in a round hole? (Assume a snug fit in both cases.)

5-2.

5-3. One real root of the equation
$$x^8 + x^6 + x^4 + x^2 = 340$$
is 2. What is the only other real root of this equation?

5-3.

5-4. In a class election, one candidate received more than 94% (but less than 100%) of the votes cast. What is the least possible number of votes cast?

5-4.

5-5. If expanded, 3^{1987} will have d more digits than 2^{1987}. If $\log_{10}2 = 0.30103$ and $\log_{10}3 = 0.47712$, what is the value of d?

5-5.

5-6. If the integers a, b, and c are all powers of 2, and if
$$a^3 + b^4 = c^5,$$
what is the least possible value of $a + b + c$?

5-6.

HIGH SCHOOL MATHEMATICS CONTESTS

Math League Press, P.O. Box 720, Tenafly, New Jersey 07670-0720

Contest Number 6   **April 7, 1987**

Name _____ Grade Level _____ Score _____

Time Limit: 30 minutes   *Answer Column*

6-1. If, for all values of x, $(x - a)^2 = (x + a)^2$, what is the value of a?

6-1.

6-2. If x is real, and $x^{64} = 64$, what is the value of x^{32}?

6-2.

6-3. What is the area of quadrilateral *ABCD* whose vertices are $A(0,3)$, $B(3,3)$, $C(5,2)$, and $D(5,0)$?

6-3.

6-4. Brian and Keith toss a fair coin 1986 and 1987 times, respectively. What is the probability that Keith gets more heads than Brian?

6-4.

6-5. A clock face has the numbers 1 through 10, equally spaced as shown. It takes 60 minutes for the minute hand to make one full 360° rotation. As the minute hand does this, the hour hand moves from one number to the next. At what exact time, between 3:00 and 4:00 on *this* clock, will the two hands coincide?

6-5.

6-6. Evaluate and simplify: $(\cos 36°)(\cos 108°)$.

6-6.

Contest Number 1   **October 27, 1987**

Name _____ Grade Level _____ Score _____

Time Limit: 30 minutes   *Answer Column*

1-1. If $a + b = 0$, but $a \neq 0$, what is the value of $\dfrac{a^{1987}}{b^{1987}}$?   1-1.

1-2. My father is 42 years old and my dog is 8. If my dog were human, it would be 56. How old would my father be if he were a dog?   1-2.

1-3. What are both values of x which satisfy $x^2 + 5|x| - 6 = 0$?   1-3.

1-4. In how many non-congruent triangles of perimeter 15 do all the sides have an integral length?   1-4.

1-5. If $a(a - 1) = b(b - 1)$, and $a \neq b$, what is the value of a explicitly in terms of b?   1-5.

1-6. In the cube at the right, each vertex is assigned two numbers, one seen and one hidden. Each number you can see is the average of the numbers hidden at the three nearest vertices. Thus, the 7 seen at vertex A is the average of the numbers hidden at vertices B, D, and E. What is the number hidden at A?

  5 E   9 H
7 A
      5 D
  9 F   5 G
3 B
      8 C

1-6.

© 1987 by Mathematics Leagues Inc.

HIGH SCHOOL MATHEMATICS CONTESTS

Math League Press, P.O. Box 720, Tenafly, New Jersey 07670-0720

Contest Number 2   December 1, 1987

Name _____ Grade Level _____ Score _____

Time Limit: 30 minutes   *Answer Column*

2-1.   What is the least positive integer $n > 1$ for which the expression $\sqrt{1+2+3+\ldots+n}$ simplifies to an integer?   2-1.

2-2.   What is the only pair of integers (x,y) for which twice the square of the first equals three times the square of the second?   2-2.

2-3.   An isosceles right triangle is removed from each corner of a square piece of paper so that a rectangle remains. What is the length of a diagonal of the rectangle if the sum of the areas of the cut-off pieces is 200?   2-3.

2-4.   The squares of two consecutive positive integers differ by 1987. What is the sum of these two integers?   2-4.

2-5.   What is the area of the region bounded by the graph of
$$|x + y| + |x - y| = 4?$$ 2-5.

2-6.   A set contains five integers. When distinct elements of this set are added together, two at a time, a complete list of different possible sums that result is: 2-6.

        637, 669, 794, 915, 919, 951, 1040, 1072, 1197.

       What is the largest of the five integers in the set?

Math League Press, P.O. Box 720, Tenafly, New Jersey 07670-0720

Contest Number 3   **January 12, 1988**

Name _____ Grade Level _____ Score _____

Time Limit: 30 minutes   *Answer Column*

3-1. What are both values of x for which $x^{1987} = x^{1988}$?   3-1.

3-2. If $\sqrt[5]{x}$ is 4, what is the value of $\sqrt{x}$?   3-2.

3-3. The area of the shaded portion of the rectangle shown is 6π, and the area of the semicircle is 18π. What is the *exact* perimeter of the rectangle?   3-3.

3-4. What are both values of x which satisfy
$$\left(\frac{1}{25}\right)^{x}(125)^{x^2} = (125)^{x}\left(\frac{1}{25}\right)?$$ 3-4.

3-5. If interest were compounded annually, what annual interest rate would (most nearly) double my money in 2 years? [Give your answer to the nearest 0.1%.]   3-5.

3-6. Suppose *ABCDE* is a positive number whose 5 digits are *A, B, C, D,* and *E.* If
$$4(ABCDE) = EDCBA,$$
what is the 5-digit number *ABCDE*?   3-6.

Contest Number 4   February 9, 1988

Name _____ Grade Level _____ Score _____

Time Limit: 30 minutes | *Answer Column*

4-1. If two of the three diameters in the diagram at the right are perpendicular, as shown, what percent of circle O is shaded? | 4-1.

4-2. If $2x^3 + 4x^2 + 6x + 8 = 2468$, and x is a positive real number, what is the value of
$$1x^3 + 9x^2 + 8x + 8?$$ | 4-2.

4-3. Two triangles are similar but not congruent; and the lengths of the sides of the first are 5, 7, and 10. The sides of the second also have integral lengths, and one of them is congruent to a side of the first. What is the perimeter of the second triangle? | 4-3.

4-4. In degrees, what are all values of x between 0° and 360° for which
$$\sin x > \sqrt{1 - \sin^2 x}?$$ | 4-4.

4-5. In the *Unlucky Lottery*, all the prizes were powers of $13, namely $1, $13, $169, etc., and the total prize money given away was $1 million. What was the least possible number of prizes in the *Unlucky Lottery*? | 4-5.

4-6. What are all ordered pairs of numbers (x,y) which satisfy
$$x^2 - xy + y^2 = 13 \quad \text{and} \quad x - xy + y = -5?$$ | 4-6.

HIGH SCHOOL MATHEMATICS CONTESTS

Math League Press, P.O. Box 720, Tenafly, New Jersey 07670-0720

Contest Number 5

March 8, 1988

Name _____ Grade Level _____ Score _____

Time Limit: 30 minutes

| | *Answer Column* |

5-1. By lines drawn parallel to its sides, a square of perimeter P is divided into 16 congruent smaller squares, each with perimeter 1. What is the value of P?

5-1.

5-2. If $x^2 = 100$, but $x^3 \neq 1000$, what is the value of x^5?

5-2.

5-3. At noon, a jar contained 81 jelly beans. If, within the first few minutes of every half-hour, one-third of the beans in the jar at the beginning of that half-hour were consumed, how many beans remained at 2 P.M.?

5-3.

5-4. What is the positive integer k for which
$$\log 1 + \log 9 + \log 8 + \log 8 = 2\log k?$$

5-4.

5-5. In the diagram, $\overline{AB}$, $\overline{AC}$, and $\overline{DE}$ are tangent to circle 0, and $m\angle A = 20°$. What is $m\angle DOE$?

5-5.

5-6. What are all real values of a for which the two values of x which satisfy
$$(a + 1)x^2 - 3ax + 4a = 0$$
are unequal numbers, each greater than 1?

5-6.

Solutions on Page 92 • Answers on Page 115

HIGH SCHOOL MATHEMATICS CONTESTS

Math League Press, P.O. Box 720, Tenafly, New Jersey 07670-0720

Contest Number 6	April 12, 1988

Name _____ Grade Level _____ Score _____

Time Limit: 30 minutes | *Answer Column*

6-1. The sum of all the positive integral factors of a certain prime number is 1988. What is this prime number?

6-1.

6-2. What are the four integral values of x for which $\frac{x}{x-2}$ has an integral value?

6-2.

6-3. If a, b, c, and d are positive integers which satisfy $\frac{a}{b} < \frac{c}{d} < 1$, arrange the 5 quantities $\frac{b}{a}, \frac{d}{c}, \frac{bd}{ac}, \frac{b+d}{a+c}$, 1 in *increasing* order.

6-3.

6-4. At the start, a jar contains only quarters and coins of lesser value. The average value of these coins is 16¢. Adding a quarter to the jar raises this average value to 17¢. What is the probability that a coin randomly selected from the jar at the start is a quarter?

6-4.

6-5. A radius of the circle drawn at the right is 6, and the two radii shown form a central angle of $x°$. The area of the shaded region (inside the circle and outside the triangle) is 32π. What is the exact value of $\sin x°$?

6-5.

6-6. What are all real values of x which satisfy

$$\sqrt{x + 2\sqrt{x-1}} + \sqrt{x - 2\sqrt{x-1}} = 2\sqrt{x-1}?$$

6-6.

Solutions on Page 93 • Answers on Page 115

37

Contest Number 1   November 1, 1988

Name _____ Grade Level _____ Score _____

Time Limit: 30 minutes   *Answer Column*

1-1. In a right triangle, the lengths of the legs are 333 and 444. What is the length of the hypotenuse?

1-1.

1-2. Ann and Bob take turns in a game. At a turn, a player takes one or two coins from a cup that at first holds six coins. The player taking the last coin wins. If Ann goes first and both play perfectly, who will win?

1-2.

1-3. On a clock with hour, minute, and second hands, the second hand is 14 cm long. In 71 minutes, the tip of the second hand travels a distance of $k\pi$ cm. What is the value of k?

1-3.

1-4. Express, as a fraction in lowest terms, the value of the following product of 99 factors:

$$\left(1 - \tfrac{1}{2}\right)\left(1 - \tfrac{1}{3}\right)\left(1 - \tfrac{1}{4}\right) \times \ldots \times \left(1 - \frac{1}{n+1}\right) \times \ldots \times \left(1 - \frac{1}{100}\right).$$

1-4.

1-5. At noon, a train leaves New York for Toronto while another leaves Toronto for New York. It takes one train 8 hours and the other 22 hours to make the trip. Both maintain constant speeds. At what time do they pass?

1-5.

1-6. What are all ordered triples of real numbers (x,y,z) which satisfy

$$\begin{aligned} (x + y)(x + y + z) &= 120, \\ (y + z)(x + y + z) &= 96, \\ (x + z)(x + y + z) &= 72? \end{aligned}$$

1-6.

© 1988 by Mathematics Leagues Inc.

Contest Number 2   **December 6, 1988**

Name _____ Grade Level _____ Score _____

Time Limit: 30 minutes   *Answer Column*

2-1. What is the value of x for which $$(1988 - x)^2 = x^2?$$	2-1.
2-2. When some people sat down to lunch, they found there was one person too many for each to sit at a separate table, so they sat two to a table and one table was left free. How many tables were there?	2-2.
2-3. What are the 3 ordered pairs of positive integers (a,b) which satisfy $$\sqrt{4^4} = a^b?$$	2-3.
2-4. Two circles are externally tangent as shown at the right. A tangent, drawn to the larger circle from the center of the smaller circle, has a length of 2. If the larger circle has a diameter of 3, what is the length of a radius of the smaller circle?	2-4.
2-5. Ten girls and five boys are in a room. At random, two of the fifteen leave the room. What is the most likely ratio of girls remaining to boys remaining?	2-5.
2-6. What are all positive integers x for which $(x - 6)(x + 14)$ is the square of an integer?	2-6.

HIGH SCHOOL MATHEMATICS CONTESTS

Math League Press, P.O. Box 720, Tenafly, New Jersey 07670-0720

Contest Number 3   January 10, 1989

Name _____ Grade Level _____ Score _____

Time Limit: 30 minutes   *Answer Column*

3-1. What is the units' digit of

$$1 + 9 + 9^2 + 9^3 + \ldots + 9^{n-1} + \ldots + 9^{1988} + 9^{1989}?$$

3-1.

3-2. Winkin said "We're all liars," Blinkin replied, "Only you are a liar," and Finkin said "You're both liars." If each of them always tells the truth or always lies, how many of the three are liars?

3-2.

3-3. What are all real values of x which satisfy

$$x + |x| = 0?$$

3-3.

3-4. Two linear functions are said to be inverses if their graphs are reflections of each other across the line $y = x$. What are the three different ordered pairs of real numbers (a,b) for which $y = ax + b$ is its own inverse?

3-4.

3-5. What is the (simplified) value of k for which the larger root of $x^2 + 4x + k = 0$ is

$$\sqrt{2+\sqrt{3}}\,\sqrt{2+\sqrt{2+\sqrt{3}}}\,\sqrt{2+\sqrt{2+\sqrt{2+\sqrt{3}}}}\,\sqrt{2-\sqrt{2+\sqrt{2+\sqrt{3}}}}?$$

3-5.

3-6. One circle has a radius of 5 and its center at (0,5). A second circle has a radius of 12 and its center at (12,0). What is the length of a radius of a third circle which passes through the center of the second circle and both points of intersection of the first 2 circles?

3-6.

© 1989 by Mathematics Leagues Inc.

40   Solutions on Page 96 • Answers on Page 116

HIGH SCHOOL MATHEMATICS CONTESTS

Math League Press, P.O. Box 720, Tenafly, New Jersey 07670-0720

Contest Number 4   **February 7, 1989**

Name _____ Grade Level _____ Score _____

Time Limit: 30 minutes   *Answer Column*

4-1. What is the only ordered triple (x,y,z) which satisfies
$$x + y + z = 9, \ \frac{1}{x} + \frac{1}{y} + \frac{1}{z} = 1, \text{ and } xy + xz + yz = 27?$$

4-1.

4-2. Although four students tried to find the sum of the first 21 positive primes, only one got the correct answer. Pat got 709, Lee got 711, Sandy got 712, and Dale got 713. Write the *name* of the person who got the correct answer.

4-2.

4-3. In a certain infinite sequence, the first 4 terms are
$$\frac{19.89}{1}, \ \frac{19.89^2}{(2)(1)}, \ \frac{19.89^3}{(3)(2)(1)}, \ \frac{19.89^4}{(4)(3)(2)(1)}, \ \cdots$$

and the nth term is $\frac{19.89^n}{n!}$. Which one of the terms in this infinite sequence has the largest numerical value? [Your answer will be an ordinal number, which is a number such as "1st," "2nd," "3rd," "4th," etc.]

4-3.

4-4. If i represents the imaginary unit, what is the only real value of k for which
$$(1 - 2i)^k = 5^k?$$

4-4.

4-5. To fill 4 big cubes, each with surface area 64, I would need n smaller cubes, each with surface area 16. What is the value of n?

4-5.

4-6. What is the ordered pair of positive integers (A,B), with B as small as possible, for which
$$\frac{7}{10} < \frac{A}{B} < \frac{11}{15}?$$

4-6.

Solutions on Page 97 • Answers on Page 116   41

HIGH SCHOOL MATHEMATICS CONTESTS

Math League Press, P.O. Box 720, Tenafly, New Jersey 07670-0720

Contest Number 5 | **March 7, 1989**

Name _____ Grade Level _____ Score _____

Time Limit: 30 minutes | *Answer Column*

5-1. Single copies of a book cost $16 each, but purchasers of 20 or more books pay only $13 per book. What are all values of $n < 20$ for which one could buy 20 books at a lower total cost than one could buy exactly n books? | 5-1.

5-2. What are both values of x which satisfy
$$1989^{10} \times 1989^{20} \times 1989^{30} \times 1989^{40} = (1989^x)^x?$$ | 5-2.

5-3. I pay for a $1 burger with 48 coins and get no change. What is the largest number of nickels I could use? | 5-3.

5-4. What is the value of $b > 0$ for which the region bounded by both the x-axis and $y = -|2x| + b$ has an area of 72? | 5-4.

5-5. The quarter-circle shown at the right has center C and radius 10. If the perimeter of rectangle $CPQR$ is 26, what is the perimeter of the shaded region? | 5-5.

5-6. What are all positive numbers x which satisfy the equation
$$\log_2 x \log_4 x \log_6 x = \log_2 x \log_4 x + \log_2 x \log_6 x + \log_4 x \log_6 x?$$ | 5-6.

Contest Number 6   April 11, 1989

Name _____ Grade Level _____ Score _____

Time Limit: 30 minutes   *Answer Column*

6-1.   What is the only positive value of b for which
$$(x + b)^2 = x^2 + 2bx + b^3$$
is an identity for all real values of x?

6-1.

6-2.   A horse and a mule, both heavily loaded, were walking side by side. When the horse complained of its load, the mule cried "What are you complaining about? If I take one sack from your back and place it on my back, my load will be twice yours; but if you take one sack from my back and place it on your back, your load will equal mine." How many sacks was the horse carrying?

6-2.

6-3.   Which is greater, $A = \sqrt{19} + \sqrt{89}$ or $B = \sqrt{18} + \sqrt{90}$?

6-3.

6-4.   In a quadrilateral which has an inscribed circle, the lengths of three consecutive sides are 4, 9, and 16 respectively. What is the length of the fourth side?

6-4.

6-5.   The principal value of $\operatorname{Arc}\sin(\cos\frac{\pi}{7})$ is $k\pi$. Express k as a reduced rational number.

6-5.

6-6.   Some workers were asked to mow two fields, one twice as big as the other. They all mowed the larger field for half a day; then they split in half. One group finished the larger field at the day's end. The others mowed the smaller field; but at day's end, there remained a part to do. This part was finished by one worker in a single day. How many workers were there?

6-6.

HIGH SCHOOL MATHEMATICS CONTESTS

Math League Press, P.O. Box 720, Tenafly, New Jersey 07670-0720

Contest Number 1   October 31, 1989

Name _____ Grade Level _____ Score _____

Time Limit: 30 minutes   *Answer Column*

1-1. A rectangle is divided into two squares by a line segment joining two of its opposite sides. If the area of one square is 36, what is the perimeter of the rectangle?

1-1.

1-2. If $r(x)$ means the reciprocal of x, what is the value of x which satisfies
$$r(x) = r(2) + r(3) + r(6)?$$

1-2.

1-3. If N is an even integer between 1 and 1989, what is the probability that N^2 is divisible by 8?

1-3.

1-4. Two vertical trees, of heights 10 and 14, are opposite each other, one on each side of a flat road. The distance between the bases of the trees is 16. A bird sits on the top of each tree. Both sight a worm somewhere between the bases of the two trees. At the same time, and with equal speeds, they both dive directly for the worm, reaching it simultaneously. What is the distance from the worm to the foot of the shorter tree?

1-4.

1-5. What are all real numbers x for which $\dfrac{3^{\sqrt{12x}} + 3}{4} = 3^{\sqrt{3x}}$?

1-5.

1-6. The product of the first n positive integers is $n!$ For example, $3! = 3 \times 2 \times 1 = 6$. What is the value of k for which
$$\frac{2000!}{1000!} = k(1 \times 3 \times 5 \times 7 \times \ldots \times 1997 \times 1999)?$$

1-6.

          Solutions on Page 100 • Answers on Page 116

HIGH SCHOOL MATHEMATICS CONTESTS

Math League Press, P.O. Box 720, Tenafly, New Jersey 07670-0720

Contest Number 2   December 5, 1989

Name _____ Grade Level _____ Score _____

Time Limit: 30 minutes   *Answer Column*

2-1.   If $A = (1-9+8+9)^{1989}$, and $B = (1-9+8-9)^{1989}$, what is the value of $(1+9+8+9)^{A+B}$?

2-1.

2-2.   If Lynn collected $10 selling 17¢ and 23¢ items, what is the least number of 17¢ items Lynn could have sold?

2-2.

2-3.   A quadrilateral has side-lengths 3, 4, 5, and x. What is the greatest possible integral value of x?

2-3.

2-4.   Each of the 20 people at a party danced at least once. Mary danced with 7 male partners, Lisa with 8, Barbara with 9, and so on up to Jill, who danced with all the male partners. With how many male partners did Jill dance?

2-4.

2-5.   What are all real numbers x for which $(x + 2)^4 + x^4 = 82$?

2-5.

2-6.   The three triangles shown have corresponding sides parallel. The one drawn between the other two has side-lengths 9, 10, and 11. The distance from each of these sides to the two sides parallel to it is 1. What is the area of the (shaded) region that is bounded between the smallest triangle and the largest triangle?

2-6.

Solutions on Page 101 • Answers on Page 116

HIGH SCHOOL MATHEMATICS CONTESTS

Math League Press, P.O. Box 720, Tenafly, New Jersey 07670-0720

Contest Number 3

January 9, 1990

Name _____ Grade Level _____ Score _____

Time Limit: 30 minutes

	Answer Column

3-1. Ali and Brian have, respectively, 20¢ and 60¢ more than Keith has. Together, the three of them have $D. If D is an integer, what is the smallest possible value of D?

3-1. _____

3-2. A rectangle is inscribed in a circle. The sum of the distances from the circle's center to the vertices of the rectangle is 40. What is the area of the circle?

3-2. _____

3-3. Whenever brothers Hocus, Pocus, and Crocus are asked a question, two lie and one tells the truth. I asked them who was youngest. Pocus said Crocus was oldest, Crocus said Hocus was youngest, and Hocus claimed not to be oldest. Who was the youngest?

3-3. _____

3-4. What are both ordered pairs of positive integers (x,y) for which

$$19x + 90y = 1990?$$

3-4. _____

3-5. What are all ordered pairs of real numbers (x,y) for which

$$5^{y-x}(x + y) = 1 \quad \text{and} \quad (x + y)^{x-y} = 5?$$

3-5. _____

3-6. What are all real values of p for which the inequality

$$-3 < \frac{x^2 + px - 2}{x^2 - x + 1} < 2$$

is satisfied by all real values of x?

3-6. _____

Solutions on Page 102 • Answers on Page 116

Contest Number 4   **February 6, 1990**

Name _____ Grade Level _____ Score _____

Time Limit: 30 minutes	*Answer Column*
4-1. If $\frac{x}{5} + \frac{x}{10} + \frac{x}{15} + \frac{x}{20} = 1 + \frac{1}{2} + \frac{1}{3} + \frac{1}{4}$, what is the value of x?	4-1.
4-2. Points A, B, C, and D lie on a straight line, but not necessarily in that order. If $AB = 3$, $BC = 4$, and $CD = 5$, what is the smallest possible value of AD?	4-2.
4-3. In a well-shuffled 52-card deck, half the cards are red and half are black. If the number of red cards in the top half is added to the number of black cards in the bottom half, the sum is 30. How many red cards are in the top half?	4-3.
4-4. What are all real numbers x for which $\left\lvert (5 - \lvert x \rvert) \right\rvert < 14$?	4-4.
4-5. What are the degree-measures of all positive acute angles x which satisfy $$\sin^2 x + \cos^2 x + \tan^2 x + \cot^2 x + \sec^2 x + \csc^2 x = 31?$$	4-5.
4-6. A parallelogram has vertices at (0,0), (2,2), (6,2), and (4,0). Point P has coordinates (1989,1990). Line t passes through point P and divides the parallelogram into two regions of equal area. What is the slope of t?	4-6.

HIGH SCHOOL MATHEMATICS CONTESTS

Math League Press, P.O. Box 720, Tenafly, New Jersey 07670-0720

Contest Number 5

March 6, 1990

Name _____ Grade Level _____ Score _____

Time Limit: 30 minutes

Answer Column

5-1. What are both ordered pairs of real numbers (a,b) which satisfy

$$(x - a)(x - b) = x^2 + 5x + 6 \text{ for all real } x?$$

5-1.

5-2. What is the sum of all three one-digit positive numbers d for which $1990 + d$ is a prime number?

5-2.

5-3. By drawing a pair of perpendicular lines through its interior, a rectangle is divided into four smaller rectangles. The areas of these smaller rectangles are x, 3, 6, and 2. What are all three possible values of x?

5-3.

5-4. At the track, my first bet doubled my money, and then I lost $1800. I bet all the money that remained and doubled my money—but then I lost $1800 again. One last time I bet it all, doubling my money, then lost $1800. This time I was broke. With how many dollars did I begin?

5-4.

5-5. The set $\{A,B,C,D,E\}$ has 32 different subsets. If Pat finds the number of elements in each subset, and then adds these 32 numbers together, what sum will Pat get?

5-5.

5-6. Determine, in simplest form, the smallest of the three numbers x, y, and z which satisfy the system

$$\log_9 x + \log_9 y + \log_3 z = 2,$$
$$\log_{16} x + \log_4 y + \log_{16} z = 1, \text{ and}$$
$$\log_5 x + \log_{25} y + \log_{25} z = 0.$$

5-6.

HIGH SCHOOL MATHEMATICS CONTESTS

Math League Press, P.O. Box 720, Tenafly, New Jersey 07670-0720

Contest Number 6	April 10, 1990

Name _____ Grade Level _____ Score _____

Time Limit: 30 minutes	Answer Column
6-1. What is the positive integer N for which $22^2 \times 55^2 = 10^2 \times N^2$?	6-1.
6-2. In a circle whose diameter is 16, two parallel chords partition the circle into four congruent arcs. What is the length of one of these chords?	6-2.
6-3. If the probability that Bob passes a driving test is p, and the probability that he fails is $6p^2$, what is the value of p?	6-3.
6-4. If the positive value of n which satisfies the equation $$\frac{1}{10} + \frac{2}{10} + \frac{3}{10} + \ldots + \frac{n}{10} = 10n?$$ is substituted back into the equation, what will be the value of the right side of this equation, $10n$?	6-4.
6-5. If I travel at 20 km/hr, I'll arrive 1 hour late. If I travel at 30 km/hr, I'll arrive 1 hour early. If I travel at k km/hr, I'll arrive just on time. What is the value of k?	6-5.
6-6. If the three cube roots of 1 are 1, ω, and ω^2, determine the value of $(1 + \omega - \omega^2)^3 + (1 - \omega + \omega^2)^3$, in simplest form as a real number.	6-6.

Solutions on Page 105 • Answers on Page 116

49

Contest Number 1   **October 30, 1990**

Name _____ Grade Level _____ Score _____

Time Limit: 30 minutes   *Answer Column*

1-1. If $(A)\left(\frac{1}{B}\right) = 1 + \frac{1}{1990}$, what is the value of $(B)\left(\frac{1}{A}\right)$?

1-1.

1-2. The sum of 20 positive numbers is what per cent of the average of these same 20 numbers?

1-2.

1-3. Three squares are lined up along the x-axis as shown, and the points with coordinates (0,4) and (21,12) are labeled accordingly. What is AB?

1-3.

1-4. In a pie-eating contest, each contestant ate a whole number of pies. The winner ate twice as many pies as the runner-up, 3 times as many as the third-place contestant, and 4 times as many as the person in fourth place. Together, these four contestants ate fewer than 60 pies. What is the greatest number of pies the winner could have eaten?

1-4.

1-5. If $x \neq y$, but $\frac{x}{y} + x = \frac{y}{x} + y$, what is the value of $\frac{1}{x} + \frac{1}{y}$?

1-5.

1-6. When Al divides each of five consecutive integers by his age, the sum of the five remainders he gets is 32. When Sue, several years older, divides each of a different set of five consecutive integers by her age, the sum of the five remainders she gets is also 32. What is the sum of the ages of Al and Sue?

1-6.

Contest Number 2   **December 4, 1990**

Name _____ Grade Level _____ Score _____

Time Limit: 30 minutes   *Answer Column*

2-1. Simplify completely:

$$(1+2+3+4+5+6+7+8+9)^{1990} - (-1-2-3-4-5-6-7-8-9)^{1990}.$$

2-1.

2-2. While I was reading Lewis Carroll's novel, *Alice in Wonderland*, I noticed that the sum of the digits of the number on the page I was reading was 19, and the sum of the digits on the next page was 2. What was the number of the page I was reading?

2-2.

2-3. What are the three ordered pairs of non-negative integers (a,b) for which

$$\sqrt{a+b} = a + b?$$

2-3.

2-4. I hiked into the woods at 4 km/h and returned by the same route at 3 km/h. If the round trip took $3\frac{1}{2}$ hrs, how many km into the woods did I hike?

2-4.

2-5. The diagonals of a rectangle intersect 8 cm farther from the shorter side than they do from the longer. If the perimeter of the rectangle is 88 cm and its area is k cm^2, what is the value of k?

2-5.

2-6. The quadratic equation $ax^2 + bx + c = 0$ has integral coefficients, and the value of its discriminant is D. What is the smallest value of $D > 48$ for which the solutions of this quadratic equation will be irrational?

2-6.

Solutions on Page 107 • Answers on Page 116

51

Contest Number 3   January 8, 1991

Name _____ Grade Level _____ Score _____

Time Limit: 30 minutes   *Answer Column*

3-1. How many two-digit whole numbers numbers contain no 0 and no more than one 1?

3-1.

3-2. Triangles *ABC* and *DCB* are both isosceles right triangles, as shown. If *AC* = 12, what is the area of triangle *BCE*?

3-2.

3-3. When 2^{1990} is multiplied by 5^{1991}, the product has 1991 digits. What is the sum of *all* these digits?

3-3.

3-4. Pat divided *x* by *y* and got a quotient of 3 and a remainder of 7. Pat then divided *x* by 2*y* and got a quotient of *q* and a remainder of *r*. If *x*, *y*, *q*, and *r* are all positive integers, what is the least possible value of *r*?

3-4.

3-5. In an arithmetic progression, the sum of the third and fifth terms is 14 and the sum of the first 12 terms is 129. If the *n*th term is 193, what is the value of *n*?

3-5.

3-6. In order, Ali, Bobby, and Carmen take turns flipping the same fair coin. The first one to toss a head wins. What is the probability that Ali wins?

3-6.

© 1991 by Mathematics Leagues Inc.

Contest Number 4   February 5, 1991

Name _____ Grade Level _____ Score _____

Time Limit: 30 minutes   *Answer Column*

4-1. All but two of my math books are titled *Algebra*, all but two are titled *Trigonometry*, and all but two are titled *Geometry*. I have at least
one math book titled *Algebra*. How many math books do I have?

4-1.

4-2. Simultaneously, two particles start
at point Q, on circle O, and move
in different directions around the
circle. If the speed of one particle is
4 times that of the other, then the
particles will next meet at point P
on the circle. If $\angle POQ$ is acute,
what is $m\angle POQ$, in degrees?

4-2.

4-3. A triangle whose area is 4 is bounded by the two coordinate axes
and also by the line whose slope is 4 and whose y-intercept is b. If
$b > 0$, what is the value of b?

4-3.

4-4. Which is larger, 1990^{1991} or 1991^{1990}?

4-4.

4-5. If f is a linear function and $f(f(x)) = 2x + 4$, what is the positive
value of $f(1)$?

4-5.

4-6. If $x = \frac{1}{2}$, then the value of the product

$$(1 + x)(1 + x^2)(1 + x^4) \times \ldots \times \left(1 + x^{2^{n-1}}\right) \times \ldots \times \left(1 + x^{128}\right)$$

is $2 - 2^k$. What is the value of k?

4-6.

Solutions on Page 109 • Answers on Page 116

53

HIGH SCHOOL MATHEMATICS CONTESTS

Math League Press, P.O. Box 720, Tenafly, New Jersey 07670-0720

Contest Number 5   **March 5, 1991**

Name _____ Grade Level _____ Score _____

Time Limit: 30 minutes   *Answer Column*

5-1.   In the entire history of Oz, each president has served exactly one 4-year term. What is the *maximum* number of presidents that could have held office in Oz during some 10-year period?

5-1.

5-2.   What are all values of x for which x and $\dfrac{17}{x}$ are both integers?

5-2.

5-3.   From point P on level ground, Alexandra observed that the angle of elevation of the top of a tower was 30°. When Alexandra moved 500 m closer to the base of the tower, to point Q, this angle from Q became 60°. If the distance from the base of the tower to point P is x m, what is the value of x?

5-3.

5-4.   If $\left(\left(\frac{5}{4}\right)^4\right)^{(5/4)^5} = \left(\left(\frac{5}{4}\right)^5\right)^x$, what is the real value of x?

5-4.

5-5.   What is the largest integral value of k for which 2^k divides the sum

$$2^{64} + 4^{32} + 8^{16} + 16^8 + 32^4 + 64^2?$$

5-5.

5-6.   What are all real numbers x for which

$$\log_{2x+4}(x^2+1) \le 1?$$

5-6.

Contest Number 6   **April 9, 1991**

Name _____ Grade Level _____ Score _____

Time Limit: 30 minutes   *Answer Column*

6-1. While reviewing the inventory of his bicycle shop, Pat noticed that, between the new bicycles and the new tricycles, there were a total of 176 wheels and 152 pedals. How many new tricycles were in Pat's shop?	6-1.
6-2. If $1992x^2 + 1991x - 1990 = 992x^2 + 991x - 990$, what is the value of $x^2 + x$?	6-2.
6-3. Each side of an isosceles right triangle is the diameter of a semicircle. What is the area of the triangle if the sum of the areas of the three semicircles is 200π?	6-3.
6-4. What is the ordered pair of numbers (x,y), with $x > y$, for which $x^2 + xy + y^2 = 84$ and $x + \sqrt{xy} + y = 14$?	6-4.
6-5. If $\cos\theta = 2\tan\theta$, what is the numerical value of $\cos^2\theta$?	6-5.
6-6. Brian has 4 pennies, 3 nickels, 2 dimes, and 2 quarters. How many different sums of money can he make using one or more of these 11 coins?	6-6.

Complete Solutions

November, 1982 — April, 1991

Contest # 1 — *Answers & Solutions* — 11/2/82

Problem 1-1

Since the expression is the expansion of $(121-21)^2$, the simplified value is $\boxed{100^2 \text{ or } 10\,000}$.

Problem 1-2

Method I: Refer to the diagram. Since the area of square $ABCD$ is 4, the area of each little square is 1 and the area of the big square is $\boxed{16}$.

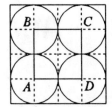

Method II: The length of each side of square $ABCD$ is 2. Also, each side equals two radii in length. Since each side of the large square equals four radii in length, the area of the large square is 16.

Problem 1-3

Method I: The number 10^{101} has 102 digits—a 1 followed by 101 zeroes. Subtracting 1, $10^{101}-1$ consists of 101 nines. The sum of the digits of this number is equal to $(9)(101) = \boxed{909}$.

Method II: $10^{101}-1 = 10^{101}-1^{101}$, which factors into $(10-1)(10^{100}+10^{99}+10^{98}+\ldots+10+1)$. The second factor is an integer of 101 digits, each of which is a 1. Finally, the sum $= 9\times101 = 909$.

Problem 1-4

An hour hand takes 60 minutes to move the 5 one-minute spaces from 4 o'clock and 5 o'clock. It has already moved 2 spaces—so it must have moved $\frac{2}{5}\times60 = 24$ minutes; and the time must be $\boxed{4:24}$.

Problem 1-5

Method I: Since 1 of every 8 marbles in Jar I is white and 1 of every 10 marbles in Jar II is white, let $40x$ (the least common multiple of 8 and 10) repre-sent the number of marbles in each jar. Hence, Jar I contains $5x$ white marbles and Jar II contains $4x$ white marbles. Since $5x + 4x = 90$, $x = 10$. There are $36x$ red marbles in Jar II, and $36\times10 = \boxed{360}$.

Method II: If k represents the number of white marbles in Jar II, there are $90-k$ white marbles in Jar I. Thus, $9k+k = 7(90-k)+(90-k)$. Solving, $k = 40$, and there are $9k = 360$ red marbles in Jar II.

Method III: Let x and y represent the number of white marbles in Jars I and II respectively. Then, $7x+x = 9y+y$. Since $x+y = 90$, $y = 40$ & $9y = 360$.

Problem 1-6

Method I: From the second of the given equations, $x+y = xy-1$. Squaring, $x^2+2xy+y^2 = x^2y^2-2xy+1$. But $x^2-xy+y^2 = 7$. Subtracting this equation from the squared equation, we get $3xy = x^2y^2-2xy-6$. Thus, $x^2y^2-5xy-6 = (xy-6)(xy+1) = 0$. From the second of the given equations, if $xy = 6$, then $x+y = 5$, and $x^2-5x+6 = 0$; but if $xy = -1$, then $x+y = -2$, and $x^2+2x-1 = 0$; so $(x,y) = \boxed{\begin{array}{c}(2,3),\ (3,2),\\(-1+\sqrt{2},-1-\sqrt{2}),\ (-1-\sqrt{2},-1+\sqrt{2})\end{array}}$.

Method II: From the 1st equation, $(x+y)^2 = 7+3xy$. From the 2nd equation, $x+y = xy-1$. Thus, $(x+y)^2 = 7+3(x+y+1)$. If $a = x+y$, then $a^2 = 7+3(a+1)$, from which $a^2-3a-10 = (a-5)(a+2) = 0$. Solving for a enables you to easily solve for x and y.

Method III: By using the substitutions $x = u + v$ and $y = u-v$, we find that $u^2+3v^2 = 7$ and $2u-u^2+v^2 = -1$. Solve the second of these equations for v^2, substitute into the first equation, and factor the result to get $2(2u-5)(u+1) = 0$. Solving, $(u,v) = (2\frac{1}{2},\pm\frac{1}{2})$, $(-1,\pm\sqrt{2})$. The values of (x,y) now follow.

[**NOTE:** The substitution $y = kx$ also works.]

Method IV: From the second equation, $y = \frac{x+1}{x-1}$. Substitution yields $x^4-3x^3-5x^2+17x-6 = 0$.

Contests written and compiled by Steven R. Conrad & Daniel Flegler   Mathematics Leagues Inc., © 1982

Problem 2-1

Since $1982^{1982} = (-1982)^{1982}$ and $N \neq 1982$, $N = \boxed{-1982}$.

Problem 2-2

Method I: If $x = 3$, the middle term is 0 and the sum of the other two terms is 4. If x does not equal 3, the middle term will have a positive value while the sum of the other two terms will be greater than or equal to 4—and the sum of

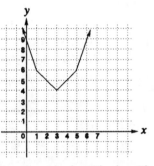

$y = |x-1| + |x-3| + |x-5|$

all three terms will be greater than 4. From the above reasoning, or from the graph above, the least value occurs when $x = 3$, and this value is $\boxed{4}$.

Method II: Since $|a| + |b| + |c| \geq |a+b+c|$, we know that $|x-1| + |x-3| + |x-5| \geq |3x-9| \geq 0$. Since $3x-9 = 0$ when $x = 3$, the sum is minimized at $x = 3$, and its value there is 4.

Problem 2-3

Since this is a percent problem in which the initial population isn't known, it is best to let $100x$ represent the initial population. During the four-year period, the year-end population went from $100x$ to $125x$ to $150x$ to $120x$ to $90x$. Since the net population decrease was $10x$, the percent decrease is $\boxed{10 \text{ or } 10\%}$.

Problem 2-4

When both sides of the given equation are multiplied by x^3, we get $1 - x - x^2 - x^3 = 0$. Rearranging, it follows that $1 = x^3 + x^2 + x$. Add 1 to each side to see that $x^3 + x^2 + x + 1 = 1 + 1 = \boxed{2}$.

Problem 2-5

Every factor of 15 and every factor of 21 must be a factor of N. Thus, 1, 3, 5, and 7 must be factors of N. Thus, 3×5, 3×7, 5×7, and $3 \times 5 \times 7$ are also factors of N. Since we've already accounted for all eight factors, N cannot have any other factors. Thus, N equals $3 \times 5 \times 7 = \boxed{105}$.

Problem 2-6

Extend $\overline{CD}$ to point G on $\overline{AB}$. Since they are inscribed in semi-circles, $\angle CED$ and $\angle CFD$ are right angles. Hence, $\overline{AF}$ and $\overline{BE}$ are altitudes of $\triangle ABC$. Since the

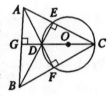

altitudes of a triangle are concurrent, $\overline{CG}$ is also an altitude—and $m\angle CGA = 90$. Since arc ED is a $50°$ arc, $m\angle ACG = 25$. In $\triangle ACG$, there is a $25°$ angle and a $90°$ angle—so $m\angle CAG = 65$. Finally, since $m\angle EAD = 50$, $m\angle DAB = \boxed{15 \text{ or } 15°}$.

Contests written and compiled by Steven R. Conrad & Daniel Flegler   Mathematics Leagues Inc., © 1982

Contest # 3

Answers & Solutions

1/11/83

Problem 3-1

By the conditions of the problem. $10t+u = 2(t+u)$, from which $u = 8t$. The only solution (in single digits) is $t = 1, u = 8$—and the number is $\boxed{18}$.

Problem 3-2

Method I: By inspection, one solution is $x = 5$. Since x and $\frac{1}{x}$ are reciprocals, a second solution will be $\frac{1}{5}$. The two answers are $\boxed{5, \frac{1}{5}}$.

Method II: Clearing fractions, we get $5x^2+5 = 25x+x$, $5x^2-26x+5 = 0$, or $(x-5)(5x-1) = 0$.

Problem 3-3

Since $17x+51y = 85$, divide by 17 to get $x+3y = 5$. Now, multiply through by 19 to get $19x+57y = \boxed{95}$.

Problem 3-4

If two angles are supplementary, then their sines are equal, while their cosines are opposites. Therefore, it follows that $\sin\frac{5\pi}{8} = \sin\frac{3\pi}{8}$, $\cos\frac{7\pi}{8} = -\cos\frac{\pi}{8}$. Thus, $\sin^2(\frac{5\pi}{8}) + \cos^2(\frac{3\pi}{8}) = \sin^2(\frac{3\pi}{8}) + \cos^2(\frac{3\pi}{8}) = 1$, and $\sin^2(\frac{\pi}{8}) + \cos^2(\frac{7\pi}{8}) = \sin^2(\frac{\pi}{8}) + \cos^2(\frac{\pi}{8}) = 1$, and the value sought is $1 + 1 = \boxed{2}$.

Problem 3-5

Method I: Draw $ABCD$ and altitude $\overline{BD}$. Since $AB = 4$ and $AD = 2$, $BD = 2\sqrt{3}$. The area of the shaded region is equal to the area of the parallelogram minus the areas of the parts of the six circles interior

to the parallelogram. Of the six parts, two are 60° sectors, two are 120° sectors, and two are 180° sectors (semicircles). In area, the six parts are equal to two full circles. The area sought is thus $\boxed{4\sqrt{3} - 2\pi}$.

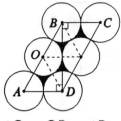

AO = OD = AD

Method II: Move the top right circle to the lower right. This merely moves the top right shaded region to the lower right. Connect the centers to form an equilateral triangle, and then subtract the areas of the sectors from this triangle.

Method III: Join the centers of 3 mutually tangent circles. One shaded region = area of an equilateral triangle - three 60° sectors. Now, multiply by 4.

Problem 3-6

Method I: Let $a = \frac{1}{2}\times\frac{3}{4}\times\frac{5}{6}\times\ldots\times\frac{99}{100}$ and then let $b = \frac{2}{3}\times\frac{4}{5}\times\frac{6}{7}\times\ldots\times\frac{98}{99}$. Multiplying, we see that $ab = \frac{1}{2}\times\frac{2}{3}\times\frac{3}{4}\times\frac{4}{5}\times\frac{5}{6}\times\ldots\times\frac{98}{99}\times\frac{99}{100}$, or $ab = \frac{1}{100}$. If a were equal to b, then the value of each would be $\frac{1}{10}$. But, $a < b$ (to prove this, multiply b by $\frac{100}{100}$ on the right, and make a factor by factor comparison between a and b). Hence, $a < \frac{1}{10}$. Also, $b > \frac{1}{10}$. Since $ab = \frac{1}{100}$ and $b < 1$, it follows that $a > \frac{1}{100}$. Thus, $\frac{1}{100} < a < \frac{1}{10}$, or $10^{-2} < a < 10^{-1}$. Therefore, $x = \boxed{-2}$.

Method II: $a = \frac{1}{2}\times\frac{3}{4}\times\frac{5}{6}\times\ldots\times\frac{99}{100} = 1(\frac{3}{2}\times\frac{5}{4}\times\frac{7}{6}\times\ldots\times\frac{99}{98})\times\frac{1}{100}$, so $a > \frac{1}{100}$. Now, $a^2 = \frac{1}{2}\times\frac{1}{2}\times\frac{3}{4}\times\frac{3}{4}\times\ldots\times\frac{99}{100}\times\frac{99}{100} = (\frac{1\times3}{2\times2}\times\frac{3\times5}{4\times4}\times\frac{5\times7}{6\times6}\times\ldots\times\frac{97\times99}{98\times98})\times\frac{1\times99}{100\times100}$, so $a^2 < 1\times\frac{1}{100}$, or $a < \frac{1}{10}$. Since $\frac{1}{100} < a < \frac{1}{10}$, $x = -2$.

Problem 4-1

Since 13 and 31, 17 and 71, and 37 and 73 are primes, the digits are the odd numbers $\boxed{1, 3, 7}$.

Problem 4-2

If $x = 2$, $t^2 + t = 2$, $(t-1)(t+2) = 0$ and $t = 1$ or -2. Since $y = t^3 + t^2$, $y = \boxed{2, -4}$.

Problem 4-3

Method I: Since the measure of an exterior angle of a regular pentagon is $\frac{360}{5} = 72$, the measure of each interior angle will be $180 - 72 = 108$. Since $90 + 108 = 198$, $m\angle CAB = 360 - 198 = 162$. Finally, since $\triangle BAC$ is isosceles, $m\angle ACB = m\angle ABC = \boxed{9 \text{ or } 9°}$.

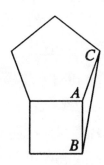

Method II: An exterior angle of a regular pentagon is $72°$ and an exterior angle of a square is $90°$, so $m\angle CAB = 90 + 72 = 162$. In $\triangle BAC$, $BA = CA$, so $m\angle ABC = 9$.

Problem 4-4

Method I: The given probabilities suggest a 6-race model, where Batman wins 1 time, Superman wins 3 times, and Wonder Woman wins 2 times. Since Superman would win 3 of the 5 times that he or Wonder Woman wins, the probability of his beating her alone would be $\boxed{\frac{3}{5}}$.

Method II: Probability $= \dfrac{\frac{1}{2}}{\frac{1}{2} + \frac{1}{3}} = \dfrac{\frac{1}{2}}{\frac{5}{6}} = \frac{3}{5}$.

Problem 4-5

If we let $x = \frac{1}{4}t$, then $2x = \frac{1}{2}t$—and then $f(2x) = f(\frac{1}{2}t)$. Hence, to find $f(\frac{1}{2}t)$, use the substitution $x = \frac{1}{4}t$ in the formula for $f(2x)$. Since $f(2x) = x^2 + 4x + 1$, $f(\frac{1}{2}t) = (\frac{1}{4}t)^2 + 4(\frac{1}{4}t) + 1 = \frac{t^2}{16} + t + 1$. Since $f(\frac{1}{2}t) = \frac{-11}{4}$, $\frac{t^2}{16} + t + 1 = \frac{-11}{4}$ or $t^2 + 16t + 60 = 0$. Therefore, $(t+6)(t+10) = 0$ and $t = \boxed{-6, -10}$.

Problem 4-6

Method I: A regular 12-gon is composed of 12 isosceles triangles of the type shown, each of which has a 30° vertex angle. If $AM = x$, then $AD = DB = 2x$, and $DM = x\sqrt{3}$. The area of each of these 12 isosceles triangles is $(\frac{1}{2}AC)(MB) = (x)(2x + x\sqrt{3})$. Since the area of the regular 12-gon is $(12)(x)(2x + x\sqrt{3}) = 24x^2 + 12x^2\sqrt{3}$, we know that $x = 1$. Hence, the perimeter $= 24x = \boxed{24}$.

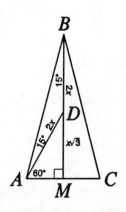

Method II: Let $AB = BC = r$ and $AC = s$. The area of $\triangle ABC = \frac{1}{2}r^2\sin 30° = \frac{1}{4}r^2$. From the given, we get $r^2 = 4(2 + \sqrt{3})$. Next, by the law of cosines, we find $s^2 = r^2 + r^2 - 2r^2\cos 30° = (2 - \sqrt{3})r^2 = (2 - \sqrt{3}) \times 4(2 + \sqrt{3}) = 4$. Thus, $s = 2$, and $P = 24$.

Problem 5-1

Since $2\sqrt{x} = 6$, $\sqrt{x} = 3$ and $x = \boxed{9}$.

Problem 5-2

Clearly, $2^0 = 1$ is the only odd integer in the sequence. Since the sequence itself is geometric, the sequence of exponents must be arithmetic, with $a_1 = 300$, $d = -2$, and $a_n = 0$. Using the formula $a_n = a_1 + (n-1)d$, we get $n = \boxed{151}$.

Problem 5-3

Since 2 and 5 are both primes less than 100, P contains 2×5 as a factor. Therefore, 10 is a factor of P and the units' digit of P must be $\boxed{0}$.

Problem 5-4

Method I: Note that $\angle A$ intercepts $\overset{\frown}{BC}$, $\overset{\frown}{CD}$, and $\overset{\frown}{DE}$, while $\angle C$ intercepts $\overset{\frown}{DE}$, $\overset{\frown}{EA}$, and $\overset{\frown}{AB}$. Since the sum of the measures of the intercepted arcs is $360° + 70° = 430°$, $m\angle A + m\angle C = \frac{430}{2} = \boxed{215 \text{ or } 215°}$.

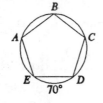

Method II: By drawing $\overline{AD}$, form inscribed quadrilateral $ABCD$. Then, $m\angle 1 + m\angle C = 180$, and $m\angle 2 = \frac{1}{2}(70) = 35$. Finally, $180 + 35 = 215$.

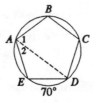

Problem 5-5

Let $f(x) = x^4 - x^3 - 18x^2 + 52x + k$. By the factor theorem, $f(2) = 40 + k = 0$, from which $k = -40$. Repeat-

ed division shows that $(x-2)$ is a triple factor of $f(x)$, the fourth factor being $(x+5)$. Therefore, the other value of r is $\boxed{-5}$.

Problem 5-6

Method I:

$\csc 20° - \cot 40°$

$= \dfrac{2\cos 20° - \cos 40°}{\sin 40°}$ (see Method II below)

$= \dfrac{2\cos(60° - 40°) - \cos 40°}{\sin 40°}$

$= \dfrac{2(\cos 60° \cos 40° + \sin 60° \sin 40°) - \cos 40°}{\sin 40°}$

$= \dfrac{\cos 40° + \sqrt{3}\sin 40° - \cos 40°}{\sin 40°}$

$= \boxed{\sqrt{3}}$.

Method II: First, convert to only sin and cos:

$\csc 20° - \cot 40° = \dfrac{1}{\sin 20°} - \dfrac{\cos 40°}{\sin 40°}$.

Next, add these fractions by converting the first into an equivalent fraction whose denominator is $\sin 40°$—but in the form $2\sin 20° \cos 20°$:

$\dfrac{1}{\sin 20°} - \dfrac{\cos 40°}{\sin 40°} = \dfrac{2\cos 20°}{2\sin 20° \cos 20°} - \dfrac{\cos 40°}{\sin 40°}$.

Get ready to use the following formula:

✿ $\cos x - \cos y = -2\sin\left(\frac{x+y}{2}\right)\sin\left(\frac{x-y}{2}\right)$.

Continuing,

$\dfrac{2\cos 20°}{2\sin 20° \cos 20°} - \dfrac{\cos 40°}{\sin 40°} = \dfrac{\cos 20° + (\cos 20° - \cos 40°)}{\sin 40°}$.

By ✿, this expression $= \dfrac{\cos 20° - 2\sin 30° \sin(-10°)}{\sin 40°} = \dfrac{\cos 20° + \sin 10°}{\sin 40°} = \dfrac{\cos 20° - \cos 100°}{\sin 40°}$.

Using the ✿ formula again, the last expression becomes $\dfrac{-2\sin 60° \sin(-40°)}{\sin 40°} = \dfrac{2\sin 60° \sin 40°}{\sin 40°} = 2\sin 60°$. Thus, $\csc 20° - \cot 40° = \sqrt{3}$.

Contests written and compiled by Steven R. Conrad & Daniel Flegler   Mathematics Leagues Inc., © 1983

Problem 6-1

Either diagonal divides the rectangle into two 6-8-10 right triangles, so the width of the rectangle is 6, its length is 8, and its perimeter is $2(6+8) = \boxed{28}$.

Problem 6-2

Using a pattern approach, expand a few powers of 5 and look for a pattern formed by the last three digits: $5^3 = 125$, $5^4 = 625$, $5^5 = 3125$, $5^6 = 15625$. If the exponent is odd, the last three digits are 125; and if the exponent is even, the last three digits are $\boxed{625}$.

Problem 6-3

First, try $a = b = c = 1$. In this case, $a^2+b^2+c^2 = 3$, but there is no integer d for which $d^2 = 3$. Next, try $a = b = 1$ and $c = 2$. In this case, $a^2+b^2+c^2 = 6$, and there is no integral value for d. Finally, try $a = 1$ and $b = c = 2$. Then $a^2+b^2+c^2 = 9 = d^2$, and $d = \boxed{3}$.

Problem 6-4

Use $\log \frac{a}{b} = \log a - \log b$ to get $\dfrac{\log\left(\frac{a}{b}\right)}{\log b} = \dfrac{\log a - \log b}{\log b} = \dfrac{\log a}{\log b} - 1 = 1000 - 1 = \boxed{999}$.

Problem 6-5

Since $\sqrt{10-x} = 6 - \sqrt{4+x}$, square both sides and rearrange terms to get $15+x = 6\sqrt{4+x}$. Square and rearrange again to get $x^2 - 6x + 81 = 0$. Now, $\sqrt{(4+x)(10-x)} = \sqrt{121 - (x^2 - 6x + 81)} = \sqrt{121 - 0} = \boxed{11}$.

[**NOTE #1:** It is incorrect to base a solution on the *invalid* conclusion that $\sqrt{a}\,\sqrt{b} = \sqrt{ab}$ is true for any numbers a and b. This "theorem" is valid only in some cases. It is valid if both a and b are positive reals. It is valid if one of the numbers is positive and one is negative. It is valid if one of the numbers is 0. It is *not* valid when both a and b are imaginary. And, in this problem, x is an imaginary number (but it can't be determined if x has the value $3+6i\sqrt{2}$ or $3-6i\sqrt{2}$), so, in this case, $\sqrt{a}\,\sqrt{b} = \sqrt{ab}$ is invalid.]

[**NOTE #2:** A typically *incorrect* solution would be: Square both sides of the original equation. The result is $4+x+2\sqrt{(4+x)(10-x)}+10-x = 36$. Simplifying, we get $\sqrt{(4+x)(10-x)} = 11$. The answer is correct —but the method is wrong!]

Problem 6-6

Method I: If (r,s,t) is a solution, then, by symmetry, (s,r,t) is also a solution, since the roles of r and s are interchangeable in the given equations. The solution will be unique if and only if $r = s$. Hence, $2r^2 = t$ and $2r+t = k$. Thus, $2r^2+2r-k = 0$. This is a quadratic equation with $a = 2$, $b = 2$, $c = -k$. This equation will have exactly one solution if and only if its discriminant is 0. Thus, $b^2-4ac = 4+8k = 0$, and $k = \boxed{-\frac{1}{2}}$.

Method II: Since $t = r^2+s^2$, rewrite the second equation as $r+s+t = r+s+r^2+s^2 = r^2+r+s^2+s = k$. By completing the square, $(r^2+r+\frac{1}{4})+(s^2+s+\frac{1}{4}) = k+\frac{1}{4}+\frac{1}{4}$, or $(r+\frac{1}{2})^2+(s+\frac{1}{2})^2 = k+\frac{1}{2}$. A unique solution exists if and only if $(r,s) = (-\frac{1}{2},-\frac{1}{2})$, in which case $k = -\frac{1}{2}$.

Contests written and compiled by Steven R. Conrad & Daniel Flegler   Mathematics Leagues Inc., © 1983

Problem 1-1

Since $23\,999\,999 = 24\,000\,000 - 1$, the time will be one hour before 9 A.M. Therefore, the time will be $\boxed{8 \text{ A.M.}}$

Problem 1-2

The measures of the two original complementary angles were 40° and 50°. When the smaller angle is increased 10%, its new measure will be 44°. To remain complementary, the other angle will need to have a measure of $90° - 44° = 46°$, which represents a decrease of $\frac{4}{50}$, or $\boxed{8\%}$.

Problem 1-3

By inspection, $2^{2^2} = 2^4 = 16$, so $x = \boxed{4}$.

[**NOTE:** In general, $\left(a^b\right)^c \neq a^{\left(b^c\right)}$, and a^{b^c} is understood to mean $a^{\left(b^c\right)}$. See, for example, p.28 of *The Lore of Large Numbers* by P. J. Davis (New Mathematical Library) or p.25 of *Mathematics and the Imagination*. It should be noted that some calculators do not handle this correctly!]

Problem 1-4

For five consecutive boxes to be shaded, the column number must be divisible by five consecutive integers, each greater than 1. Thus, the column number must be divisible by 2, 3, 4, 5, and 6. Among the integers from 1 to 100, the only such column number is $\boxed{60}$.

Problem 1-5

Method I: In the diagram, let $\overline{OR}$ and $\overline{OQ}$ be perpendicular to the sides of the rectangle, as shown. If $OR = OQ$ 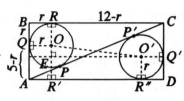 $= r$, then $AQ = 5-r$ and $CR = 12-r$. Since $AP = AQ$ and $CP = CR$, $AP+PC = 5-r+12-r = 17-2r$. Since $AC = 13 = 17-2r$, $r = 2$. In right triangle OEO', $OE = 5-2r = 1$ and $EO' = 12-2r$, so $OO' = \boxed{\sqrt{65}}$.

Method II: As above, $r = 2$. Placing the lower right-hand corner of the rectangle at the origin, one center is at $(2,3)$ and the other is at $(10,2)$. By the distance formula, $d = \sqrt{65}$. [**NOTE:** Alternatively, $r = A \div \frac{1}{2}P$, where $\frac{1}{2}P$ is half the perimeter.]

Method III: Draw $\overline{O'C}$, $\overline{O'D}$, and $\overline{O'A}$. Since the area of $\triangle ADC$ is equal to the sum of the areas of $\triangle ADO'$, $\triangle DCO'$, and $\triangle CAO'$, $30 = 12r/2 + 5r/2 + 3r/2$, and $r = 2$. Continue as above.

Problem 1-6

Subtracting the second equation from the first, $(y-z)(1-x) = 0$. Subtracting the third equation from the first, $(x-z)(y-1) = 0$. There are four possibilities: (1) $y-z = 0 = x-z$, (2) $y-z = 0 = y-1$, (3) $1-x = 0 = x-z$, and (4) $1-x = 0 = y-1$. From the first case, $x = y = z$. Therefore, $x+x^2 = 12$ and $x = y = z = 3$ or $x = y = z = -4$. The other 3 cases produce the other three solutions, and the solutions are:

$\boxed{(3,3,3),\ (-4,-4,-4),\ (1,1,11),\ (1,11,1) \text{ and } (11,1,1)}$.

Contests written and compiled by Steven R. Conrad & Daniel Flegler   Mathematics Leagues Inc., © 1983

Problem 2-1

The square root dates are 1/1/01, 2/2/04, 3/3/09, 4/4/16, 5/5/25, 6/6/36, 7/7/49, 8/8/64, and 9/9/81. The total number of such dates is $\boxed{9}$.

Problem 2-2

Draw $\overline{AC}$. Since $AB = BC = AC$, $\triangle ABC$ is equilateral. Therefore, $m\angle ABC = \boxed{60 \text{ or } 60°}$.

Problem 2-3

The first inequality is equivalent to $x^2 - 2x - 8 \le 0$, while the second is equivalent to $x^2 - 2x - 8 \ge 0$. Since their intersection is $x^2 - 2x - 8 = 0$, or $(x+2)(x-4) = 0$, it follows that $x = \boxed{-2, 4}$.

Problem 2-4

Let $C = 1 + 2 + 3 + \ldots + 1983$. Thus, $A = (1983) \times (C + 1984) = 1983C + 1983(1984)$, and $B = (1983 + 1)C = 1983C + C$. Thus, A would be greater than B if $1983(1984)$ were greater than C. But, C is less than $1983 + 1983 + \ldots + 1983 = 1983(1983)$, so the larger one is $\boxed{A}$.

[**NOTE:** The inequality can also be established by summing the arithmetic progressions.]

Problem 2-5

Let $\overline{BM}$ be the median to $\overline{AC}$. Since the perimeter of $\triangle ABM$ is equal to the perimeter of $\triangle CBM$, $AB = BC$, and $\triangle ABC$ is isosceles. The median to the

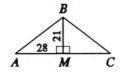

base of an isosceles triangle is also an altitude, so $\overline{BM} \perp \overline{AC}$. By the Pythagorean theorem, $AB = 35$, so the perimeter of $\triangle ABC = 35 + 35 + 56 = \boxed{126}$.

[**NOTE:** In ABC, the length of the median m to side c is given by the formula $m_c = \frac{1}{2}\sqrt{2(a^2 + b^2) - c^2}$.]

Problem 2-6

Method I: Let $P(n)$ denote the probability that the 13th heart is drawn on the nth card. Then, $P(52) = \frac{1}{4}$ since each of the four suits is equally likely to be the last card. Since we know that $P(51) = P(\text{the } 52\text{nd card } isn't \text{ a heart}) \times P(51\text{st card is a heart}) = (\frac{3}{4})(\frac{13}{51}) = \frac{39}{204}$, we find $P(52)$ is greater than $P(51)$. Similarly, we find that $P(50) = (\frac{3}{4})(\frac{38}{51})(\frac{13}{50})$. In fact, $P(n)$ decreases as n decreases. Therefore, the answer is $\boxed{52 \text{ or } 52\text{nd or "last"}}$.

Method II: Let $T(n)$ denote the probability that the nth card is the 12th heart. Notice that the 12th heart can fall in any of the positions 12 to 51. If, say, card 30 were the 12th heart, then the 13th heart could fall in any of the positions 31 through 52. In this case, positions 31 through 52 each have probability $[\frac{1}{22}][T(30)]$ of being the location of the 13th heart. Thus, $P(52)$ equals the sum of the 39 numbers $[\frac{1}{40}][T(12)] + \ldots + [\frac{1}{1}][T(51)]$. Similarly, $P(51)$ is the sum of only the first 38 of those same 39 numbers, $P(50)$ is the sum of only the first 37 of those 39 numbers, etc. In general, the probabilities continue to decrease.

[**NOTE:** The probability of the 13th heart occurring in position k is proportional to the number of ways of arranging the other 12 hearts and $k-13$ non-hearts in the previous $k-1$ positions. The value of this function increases as the value of k increases.]

Contests written and compiled by Steven R. Conrad & Daniel Flegler   **Mathematics Leagues Inc., © 1983**

Problem 3-1

Let a and b represent the length and width of the rectangle. Then $2a^2 + 2b^2 = 100$, or $a^2 + b^2 = 50$. The length of the diagonal is $\boxed{\sqrt{50} \text{ or } 5\sqrt{2}}$.

Problem 3-2

If $2^4 + a^b = 2^5$, $a^b = 16$. Since there are only three solutions to this equation, $ab = 16^1$ or 4^2 or 2^4, so $(a,b) = \boxed{(16,1), (4,2), (2,4)}$.

Problem 3-3

Since n can be positive, negative, or zero, the possible values of n are 0, ± 1, ± 2, ± 3, ± 4, ± 5, ± 6, ± 7, ± 8, ± 9, and ± 10, a total of $\boxed{21}$ values.

Problem 3-4

Method I: Since Harold began with $20, after just one hour he had $40. Therefore, it took Harold an additional 19 hours to amass his fortune. Horace began with $40, so he took $\boxed{19}$ hours.

Method II: The series of hourly earnings of the Greedy brothers form two geometric series, each with $r = 2$. Since $20 \times 2^{19} = 40 \times 2^{n-1}$, $n = 19$.

Problem 3-5

Since x must have a value between 5 and 6, it is clear that $[x] = 5$. Thus, $(x)(5) = 28$, and $x = \boxed{\dfrac{28}{5}}$.

Problem 3-6

Method I: Division of $x^3 + 6x^2 + 12x + 24$ by $x+2$ produces a quotient of $(x+2)^2$ and a remainder of 16, so $(x+2)^3 + 16 = 0$. Therefore, $(x+2)^3 = -16$, and $x = \boxed{-2 + \sqrt[3]{-16}}$.

Method II: The equation can be rewritten as $(x+2)^3 = -16$. To develop this form, rewrite the equation in stages, then use the binomial theorem to write the equation in the new form. Since $x^3 + 6x^2 + 12x + 24 = 0$, we find that $x^3 + 3(x^2)(2) + 3(x)(2^2) + 2^3 = -16$, or $(x+2)^3 = -16$. Therefore, $x = -2 + \sqrt[3]{-16}$.

Contests written and compiled by Steven R. Conrad & Daniel Flegler   Mathematics Leagues Inc., © 1984

Problem 4-1

$N = 2 \times 3 \times 5 \times 7 \times 11 \times 13 \times 10^6$, so the least prime number which is *not* a factor of N is $\boxed{17}$.

Problem 4-2

If each leg were x, then the base would be $2x$. Since the sum of any two sides of a triangle must be greater than the third side, this cannot be the correct assignment of lengths. Hence, each leg is $2x$ and the base is x. Thus $x + 2x + 2x = 40$, $x = 8$, and $AB = \boxed{16}$.

Problem 4-3

Since there is a 4-unit distance from $(-1,0)$ to $(3,0)$, each of the 1000 congruent segments must be $\frac{4}{1000}$ of a unit in length. Hence, the 60th division point occurs $60 \times \frac{4}{1000} = \frac{24}{100}$ of a unit to the right of $(-1,0)$. Consequently, the coordinates of the point P_{60} are $(-1 + \frac{24}{100}, 0) = \boxed{\left(\frac{-76}{100}, 0\right) \text{ or } \left(\frac{-19}{25}, 0\right)}$.

Problem 4-4

Rearranging, $x^2 + 1 = \cos x$. The left side of this equation is always greater than or equal to 1, while the right side is always less than or equal to 1. For equality, both sides must equal 1, so $x = \boxed{0}$.

Problem 4-5

Clearing fractions, we get $7x + 7yi + xi - y = 7 + 7i$. Grouping, $(7x - y) + (x + 7y)i = 7 + 7i$. Now, equate real and imaginary parts to get $7x - y = 7$ and $x + 7y = 7$. Solving, $x = \frac{28}{25}$ and $y = \frac{21}{25}$. Therefore, $x + y = \boxed{\frac{49}{25}}$.

Problem 4-6

The equation $\sqrt{x} = \sqrt{a} + \sqrt{b}$ has a solution in positive integers if and only if x contains a perfect square factor.* For example, $\sqrt{9} = \sqrt{4} + \sqrt{1}$ or $\sqrt{18} = \sqrt{9 \cdot 2} = 3\sqrt{2} = \sqrt{2} + 2\sqrt{2} = \sqrt{2} + \sqrt{8}$. There are 250 values of $x \le 1000$ that contain a factor of 4. Similarly, the number of values of $x \le 1000$ that (respectively) contain a factor of 3^2, 5^2, 7^2, 11^2, 13^2, 17^2, 19^2, 23^2, 29^2, and 31^2 is 111, 40, 20, 8, 5, 3, 2, 1, 1, and 1—for a total of 442 values. But, some of these values, such as 36, have been counted twice—once as a multiple of 2^2 and once as a multiple of 3^2. We must count the number of such duplications and subtract them from our total. The number of values of $x \le 1000$ that respectively contain a factor of $2^2 3^2$, $2^2 5^2$, $2^2 7^2$, $2^2 11^2$, $2^2 13^2$, $3^2 5^2$, and $3^2 7^2$ are 27, 10, 5, 2, 1, 4, and 2—a total of 51 such duplications. Finally there is the case of $2^2 3^2 5^2$. This was counted 3 times in the first group—and was then deleted 3 times in the second group (for $2^2 3^2$, $2^2 5^2$, and $3^2 5^2$). Thus, the answer is $442 - 51 + 1 = \boxed{392}$.

*[**NOTE:** Let's prove that there is a solution in positive integers if and only if x contains a perfect square factor. Since $\sqrt{x} = \sqrt{a} + \sqrt{b}$, $x = a + b + \sqrt{ab}$. For x to be an integer, ab must be a square. If the prime factorization of a has a prime factor to an odd power, then b must also have that same prime factor also to an odd power (and *vice-versa*). Thus, when a is simplified, say into the form $u\sqrt{v}$, then b must simplify into the form $w\sqrt{v}$. Therefore, $\sqrt{x} = u\sqrt{v} + w\sqrt{v} = (u+w)\sqrt{v}$, and $\sqrt{x}$ **must** be of this form. Thus, $x = (u+w)^2 v$, and x is a square or a multiple of a square.]

Contests written and compiled by Steven R. Conrad & Daniel Flegler   Mathematics Leagues Inc., © 1984

Problem 5-1

Method I: Divide 90 successively by 11, 12, 13, ... The first time that the remainder becomes 10 is when 90 is divided by $\boxed{16}$.

Method II: Since 80 is 10 less than 90, it leaves a remainder of 10 when divided into 90. The smallest positive integer that leaves a remainder of 10 when divided into 90 must be greater than 10 *and* a factor of 80. The factors of 80 are 1, 2, 4, 5, 8, 10, 16, 20, 40, and 80; the smallest factor greater than 10 is 16.

Problem 5-2

Draw $\overline{CD}$. This divides $\triangle ABC$ into four congruent triangles. Each triangle has an area of 6. The rectangle contains two of these triangles, so the area of the rectangle is $\boxed{12}$.

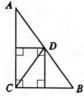

Problem 5-3

Method I: By the triangle–length inequality, each of the following six inequalities must be satisfied: $3+4 > x$, $3+x > 4$, $4+x > 3$, $9+16 > x^2$, $9+x^2 > 16$. and $16+x^2 > 9$. The only integral values of x which satisfy all six inequalities are $\boxed{3, 4}$.

Method II: If the triangle's sides are a, b, and x, then $a-b < x < a+b$, so $1 < x < 7$ and $7 < x^2 < 25$. For x to be integral, $x = 3$ or 4.

Problem 5-4

If Methuselah had worked forever, he would have earned $\$20\,000 + \$10\,000 + \$5\,000 + \ldots$. These earnings form an infinite geometric progression whose sum S is given by the formula $S = \frac{a}{1-r} = \$40\,000$. Although this sum is not identical to the amount he actually earned in 900 years, it differs from that amount by less than 50¢. Thus, to the nearest dollar, he earned $\boxed{\$40\,000}$.

[**NOTE:** To the nearest dollar, the $\$40\,000$ was earned by the 17th day!]

Problem 5-5

Since both p and q are positive, $\log_2 p + \log_2 q = \log_2 pq$. But p and q are roots of the quadratic equation, $2x^2 - 5x + 1 = 0$, so $pq =$ the product of the roots of this equation $= \frac{c}{a} = \frac{1}{2}$, and $\log_2 pq = \log_2 \frac{1}{2} = \boxed{-1}$.

Problem 5-6

Note that $5+2\sqrt{6} = (\sqrt{3}+\sqrt{2})^2$, and that $5-2\sqrt{6} = (\sqrt{3}-\sqrt{2})^2$, and also that $\sqrt{3}-\sqrt{2} = (\sqrt{3}+\sqrt{2})^{-1}$. Let $y = 2\sin x$. The original equation can now be rewritten as $(\sqrt{3}+\sqrt{2})^y + (\sqrt{3}+\sqrt{2})^{-y} = 2\sqrt{3}$. Now, let $(\sqrt{3}+\sqrt{2})^y = b$. Then, $b + b^{-1} = 2\sqrt{3}$. Simplifying, $b^2 - 2b\sqrt{3} + 1 = 0$. Solving for b, $b = \sqrt{3} \pm \sqrt{2}$. Hence, $y = \pm 1$, from which $\sin x = \pm\frac{1}{2}$, and, finally, $x = \boxed{30°, 150°, 210°, \text{ and } 330°}$.

Contests written and compiled by Steven R. Conrad & Daniel Flegler   Mathematics Leagues Inc., © 1984

Problem 6-1

If $\frac{3+x}{4+x} = \frac{6+x}{8+x}$, then $x^2+11x+24 = x^2+10x+24$, from which $x = \boxed{0}$.

Problem 6-2

Method I: $\frac{4444^4}{2222^4} = \left(\frac{4444}{2222}\right)^4 = 2^4 = \boxed{16}$.

Method II: $4444^4 = (2 \times 2222)^4 = 2^4 \times 2222^4$, so the fraction reduces to $2^4 = 16$.

Problem 6-3

If $x^{100} = 2x^{50}$, then $x^{50}(x^{50}-2) = 0$ and $x^{50} = 0$ or $x^{50} = 2$. Thus, $x^{200} = \boxed{0 \text{ or } 16}$.

Problem 6-4

Method I: The sum of the squares of two real numbers can equal 0 if and only if each has the value 0. Thus, $x+y-5 = 0$, $x-y-1 = 0$, and $(x,y) = \boxed{(3,2)}$.

Method II: When expanded and rearranged, the given equation can be rewritten as $(x-3)^2 + (y-2)^2 = 0$, which is a (degenerate) point circle, (3,2).

Problem 6-5

If $\sin P = \sin Q$, and P and Q are angles of a convex quadrilateral, then either $P = Q$ or $P = 180°-Q$. The given lengths are not equal, so the quadrilateral cannot be a rectangle with four congruent angles. Let one of the angles have a measure of y. Then, the measures of the other angles must be y, $180°-y$, and $180°-y$. If the opposite angles were congruent, the quadrilateral would be a parallelogram, so the quadrilateral must be an isosceles trapezoid, and the value of x, (the length of the fourth side) may be any of the numbers $\boxed{5, 6, 7}$.

Problem 6-6

Method I: Extend radius $\overline{CO}$ to point C' on the circle, creating diameter $\overline{C'OC}$. At point C', draw a tangent to the circle, meeting $\overline{AB}$ (extended) at J. Now, $HJ = 8+6+8 = 22 = C'OC$, so $CO = 11$, and the area of the circle is $\boxed{121\pi}$.

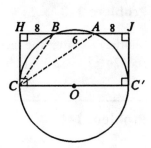

Method II: The perpendicular drawn from the center of the circle to $\overline{AB}$ bisects $\overline{AB}$ into two segments of length 3. Since the distance from H to the foot of this perpendicular is 11, the length of a radius is 11—and the area of the circle is 121π.

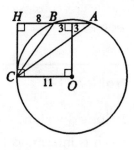

Contests written and compiled by Steven R. Conrad & Daniel Flegler   Mathematics Leagues Inc., © 1984

Problem 1-1

Since $32 \times 31 = 992$, the answer is a multiple of 992. The only multiple of 992 in the interval from 1500 to 2500 is $\boxed{1984}$.

Problem 1-2

The two outer regions are congruent. The sum of their areas is 24π, so each has an area of 12π, and the area of each circle is 36π. Since the length of a radius is 6, the circumference is $\boxed{12\pi}$.

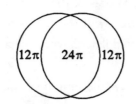

Problem 1-3

Multiply together the factors on the left, and you get $2^{24} - 24^{-24} = (2^3)^8 - (2^3)^{-8} = 8^8 - 8^{-8}$, so $x = \boxed{8}$.

Problem 1-4

Taken together, my parents' 4 children account for 4 of the 10 maternal grandchildren. Thus, only 6 of the 10 maternal grandchildren are my first cousins. Similarly, only $11 - 4 = 7$ of the 11 paternal grandchildren are my first cousins. Therefore, my first cousins number $6 + 7 = \boxed{13}$.

Problem 1-5

By long division, $\dfrac{n^3 - 12}{n - 4} = n^2 + 4n + 16 + \dfrac{52}{n - 4}$, which is integral as long as $n-4$ is a divisor of 52. The positive divisors of 52 are 1, 2, 4, 13, 26, and 52.

Setting $n-4$ equal, in turn, to 1, 2, 4, 13, 26, and 52, we find that $n = \boxed{5, 6, 8, 17, 30, \text{ and } 56}$.

Problem 1-6

Method I: Since r is a root of $x^4 - x^3 + x^2 - x + 1 = 0$, r is also a root of $(x + 1)(x^4 - x^3 + x^2 - x + 1) = 0$. But $(x + 1)(x^4 - x^3 + x^2 - x + 1) = x^5 + 1$, so r satisfies $x^5 + 1 = 0$. Therefore, $r^5 + 1 = 0$, or $r^5 = -1$. It then follows that $r^{40} - r^{30} + r^{20} - r^{10} + 1 = (r^5)^8 - (r^5)^6 + (r^5)^4 - (r^5)^2 + 1 = (-1)^8 - (-1)^6 + (-1)^4 - (-1)^2 + 1 = \boxed{1}$.

Method II: This solution will clarify why the first solution does *not* claim that $r = -1$ is a solution of the original equation. The original equation is a finite geometric series with first term x^4 and common ratio $-1/x$. Summing this series, we get $x^4 - x^3 + x^2 - x + 1 = 0$ is equivalent to $(x^5 + 1)/(x + 1) = 0$—and therefore $x \neq -1$. By DeMoivre's Theorem, the five roots of $x^5 + 1 = 0$ (one of which, -1, is not a root of our original equation) are $r_1 = 1 \operatorname{cis} 36°$, $r_2 = 1 \operatorname{cis} 108°$, $r_3 = 1 \operatorname{cis} 180° = -1 + 0i$, $r_4 = 1 \operatorname{cis} 252°$, and $r_5 = 1 \operatorname{cis} 324°$, where r_3 is *not* a root, but r_1, r_2, r_4, and r_5 are the roots of $x^4 - x^3 + x^2 - x + 1 = 0$. Since $36°$, $108°$, $252°$, and $324°$ are all multiples of $36°$, multiplying each by 10 will yield multiples of $360°$. Thus, r^{40}, r^{30}, r^{20}, and r^{10} are all equal, and $r^{40} - r^{30} + r^{20} - r^{10} + 1 = 1$. This method not only solves the problem, but it also reveals the 4 different values of r that satisfy the original equation.

Problem 2-1

Since each of the first five fractions on the left side has a value of $\frac{1}{5}$, the sum of these five fractions is 1, and the value of x must be $\boxed{0}$.

Problem 2-2

The odd number 111 111 111 111 is not divisible by 2. Since the sum of its digits is 12 (a number divisible by 3), the number itself must be divisible by 3. Thus, the largest proper integral factor of 111 111 111 111 must be 111 111 111 111 ÷ 3 = $\boxed{37\,037\,037\,037}$.

Problem 2-3

During each 12-hour period, there are only 11 bell chimes. The bell chimes when the hour hand is between 12 and 1 (and the minute hand is pointing in the exact opposite direction). Similarly, there is a chime between 1 and 2, 2 and 3, 3 and 4, and 4 and 5. The first time after 5 that the hands form a 180° angle is at precisely 6 o'clock, so there is no chime between 5 and 6. Thus, in the given 24-hour period, the number of chimes heard will be $\boxed{22}$.

Problem 2-4

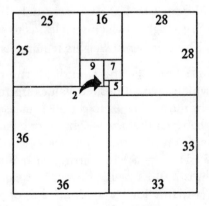

Method I: The pictured rectangle is a "perfect squared rectangle." Its perimeter is $\boxed{260}$.

Method II: Adding together the areas of the squares, the total area of the rectangle is $2^2 + 5^2 + \ldots + 33^2 + 36^2 = 4209 = 3 \times 23 \times 61$ (the prime factorization). Since the side-length of one of the squares is 36, each dimension of the rectangle must be at least 36. Thus, the dimensions of the rectangle must be 69 by 61, making its perimeter 260.

Problem 2-5

Method I: Rearranging and factoring, we get $x(y+6-x) = 11$. Since both x and y are positive integers, $x = 1$ or $x = 11$ and $(x,y) = \boxed{(1,6),\ (11,6)}$.

Method II: Since x and y are positive integers and $y = x - 6 + 11/x$, $x = 1$ or 11, and $y = 6$.

Problem 2-6

Method I: An altitude is 12 and $\triangle\text{I} \sim \triangle\text{III}$, so call the segments of the altitude $12x$ and $12y$ (with $x+y = 1$), and call the segments of the given diagonal $15x$ and $15y$. By the Pythagorean Theorem, we get the segment lengths marked $9x$ and $9y$.

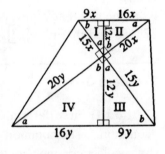

Angles a and b are complementary, so all numbered triangles are similar; and the lengths $16x$, $20x$, $16y$, and $20y$ are as shown. The trapezoid's area equals $\frac{1}{2}(12)(25x+25y) = 6(25)(x+y) = 6(25)(1) = \boxed{150}$.

Method II: Let $A(0,0)$, $B(b,12)$, $C(c,12)$, $D(a,0)$ be the vertices of the trapezoid and let $BD = 15$. Thus, $a-b = 9$ (assume $a > b$ without loss of generality). Since the product of the slopes is -1, we get $c = 16$. The area = $\frac{1}{2}(12)(AD+BC) = 6[(b+9)+(16-b)] = 6 \times 25 = 150$.

Contests written and compiled by Steven R. Conrad & Daniel Flegler · Mathematics Leagues Inc., © 1984

Problem 3-1

Since $x^2 = x^x$, either the exponents are equal or the value of the base is 1. Therefore, $x = \boxed{1, 2}$.

Problem 3-2

Using fractional exponents, the given can be easily rewritten as $1985^{\frac{1}{2}} \times 1985^{\frac{1}{3}} \times 1985^{\frac{1}{6}}$. By adding the exponents, we see that this product equals $1985^{\frac{1}{2}+\frac{1}{3}+\frac{1}{6}}$ $= 1985^1$, whose value is $\boxed{1985}$.

Problem 3-3

Since $n!$ has 23 as a factor, but does not have 29 as a factor, it is clear that $23 \leq n \leq 29$. There are 4 factors of 7 in $n!$, so the first 4 multiples of 7, namely 7, 14, 21, and 28, must be concurrent factors of $n!$. From the fact that 7^4 divides 28!, but does not divide 27!, we find that $n = \boxed{28}$.

Problem 3-4

Method I: First determine which pair of sides is "common." The common pair will be the pair with the smallest common multiple. If $[a,b]$ denotes the least common multiple of a and b, then $[5,4] = 20$, $[5,9] = 45$, $[5,11] = 55$, $[6,4] = 12$, $[6,9] = 18$, $[6,11] = 66$, $[7,4] = 28$, $[7,9] = 63$, $[7,11] = 77$. Thus, the lengths of the sides of the first triangle are 10, 12, 14 while the those of the second are 12, 27, and 33. The least possible common side is $\boxed{12}$.

Method II: The first $\triangle$ is from (5,6,7), (10,12,14), (15,18,21), . . . while the second is from (4,9,11), (8,18,22), (12,27,33), . . . The answer is 12.

Problem 3-5

Method I: The system will fail to have a unique solution if and only if one equation is a linear combination of the other two. Subtract the second equation from the third to get $x-2y-5z = 0$. This will be identical to the first equation if and only if $k = \boxed{-5}$. [Or, the sum of the first two equations will be the same as the third equation when $k = -5$.]

Method II: Use determinants.

Problem 3-6

Method I: *If* weights were allowed on only one side of the balance, the weights needed would be 1g, 2g, 4g, 8g, 16g, 32g, 64g. To measure a weight of Ng, use only the weights represented by the digit 1 in base 2. *But* with weights allowed in either pan, it is most efficient to first represent N in base 3, where the only possible digits are 0, 1, 2. By replacing each 2 with a $(3-1)$, we'll see how any number can be expressed as the sum or *difference* of powers of 3. Thus $23 = (2)3^2+(1)3+2 = (3-1)3^2+(1)3+(3-1) = 3^3-3^2+(2)3-1 = 3^3-3^2+(3-1)3-1 = 3^3-3-1$. Thus, to measure 23g, place weight 3^3g in one pan and weights 3g and 1g in the other. [A slightly quicker equivalent rule is: starting at the left, replace any 2 by a -1—and increase the digit to the immediate left by 1. This procedure may need repeating.] To measure any N from 1 to 100, we'd need only 1g, 3g, 9g, 27g, and 81g weights (which enables us to weigh up to 121g). The number of weights required is $\boxed{5}$.

Method II: Let \$ be the sum of all the previous weights which give all desired values up to \$. The next weight must allow us to get \$+1, measured as a *difference* between the new weight on one pan and all the others, \$, on the other. The new weight is 2\$+1, since $(2\$+1)-\$ = \$+1$. Starting with \$ = 0, the first weight is $2(0)+1 = 1$. The second weight is $2(1)+1 = 3$ [which allows weighing 1,2,3, or 4 units], the third weight is $2(1+3)+1 = 2(4)+1 = 9$, etc.

Contests written and compiled by Steven R. Conrad & Daniel Flegler   Mathematics Leagues Inc., © 1985

Problem 4-1

The sum of the two shortest sides is greater than the longest side, and (since it's integral) the longest side is at least 1 more than either of the other two sides. Thus, the shortest side must be greater than 1. Since a triangle with sides of 2, 3, and 4 does exist, the minimum length of the shortest side is $\boxed{2}$.

Problem 4-2

The difference of the numbers on the left side of the equation is the odd number 41. Therefore, one of the terms on the left side must be even and the other must be odd. Since $104y$ is even, $187x$ must be odd, and therefore x must be odd. The only pair in which x is not odd is $\boxed{(314,565)}$.

Problem 4-3

Method I: Al's equation is $k_1(x+2)(2x+3) = k_1(2x^2+7x+6) = 0$. Barb's equation is $k_2(x-2)(x-3) = k_2(x^2-5x+6) = 0$. Since $C = 6$ in both equations, the k's are equal and the correct equation is $k(x^2+7x+6) = 0$, whose solutions are $\boxed{-1,\ -6}$.

Method II: Al's equation could be $2x^2+7x+6 = 0$, and Barbara's could be $x^2-5x+6 = 0$. From the given information, we can see that the correct equation would be $x^2 + 7x + 6 = 0$.

Problem 4-4

The three equations can be rewritten as $|y| = y$, $|x-3| = -(x-3)$, and $|y-x| = -(y-x)$. From the first of these, $y \geq 0$. From the other two, $x \leq 3$ and $y \leq x$. From the graph of the system, we can determine that the number of lattice points (points with two integral coordinates) on the graph is $\boxed{10}$.

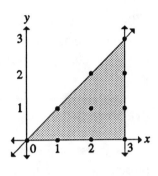

Problem 4-5

By the formula for the sum of an infinite geometric series, we find $S = \dfrac{a_1}{1-r} = \dfrac{\frac{a}{b}}{1-\frac{1}{b}} = \dfrac{a}{b-1} = \dfrac{1}{3} = \dfrac{2}{6} = \dfrac{3}{9} = \dots$. Only for $\frac{1}{3}$ and $\frac{2}{6}$ does b have a one-digit value, so $\dfrac{a}{b} = \boxed{\dfrac{1}{4},\ \dfrac{2}{7}}$.

Problem 4-6

Since 2 is a solution, the product $= (2-a)(2-b)(2-c)(2-d) = 9$. Since $a, b, c,$ and d are different integers, all 4 of the factors on the left side must have different values. Therefore, $(2-a)(2-b)(2-c)(2-d) = (3)(-3)(1)(-1)$. Hence, $(2-a)+(2-b)+(2-c)+(2-d) = 3-3+1-1$. It follows from this that $8-(a+b+c+d) = 0$, and $a+b+c+d = \boxed{8}$.

Contests written and compiled by Steven R. Conrad & Daniel Flegler   Mathematics Leagues Inc., © 1985

Problem 5-1

When 1985 is divided by 19, there is a quotient of 104 and a remainder of 9, so the number of the soldier who called out 1985 was $\boxed{9}$.

Problem 5-2

The smallest of the three integers will be as large as possible when the three integers are as nearly equal as possible. Since $720 = 8 \times 9 \times 10$, the largest possible value of x is $\boxed{8}$.

Problem 5-3

Method I: The numerator $= 5^2(1^2 + 2^2 + \ldots + 19^2 + 20^2)$, so the value of the quotient is $\boxed{25}$.

Method II: If $\frac{a}{b} = \frac{c}{d} = \frac{e}{f} = \ldots = x$, then $x = \frac{a + c + e + \ldots}{b + d + f + \ldots}$, so the quotient equals $\frac{5^2}{1^2} = 25$.

Problem 5-4

Rationalizing the denominator of each fraction, the sum is $\frac{\sqrt{3} - \sqrt{1}}{2} + \frac{\sqrt{5} - \sqrt{3}}{2} + \frac{\sqrt{7} - \sqrt{5}}{2} + \frac{\sqrt{9} - \sqrt{7}}{2} = \frac{\sqrt{9} - \sqrt{1}}{2} = \boxed{1}$.

Problem 5-5

Since $\log_{\frac{1}{2}}(\sin^2 x \cos^2 x) = 3$, $(\sin x \cos x)^2 = \frac{1}{8}$. Therefore, $(2 \sin x \cos x)^2 = \frac{1}{2}$, $\sin 2x = \pm \frac{1}{\sqrt{2}}$, $2x = \frac{\pi}{4}, \frac{3\pi}{4}, \frac{5\pi}{4}, \frac{7\pi}{4}, \ldots$. Since $0 \le x \le \pi$, $x = \boxed{\frac{\pi}{8}, \frac{3\pi}{8}, \frac{5\pi}{8}, \frac{7\pi}{8}}$.

Problem 5-6

Method I: If the sides of the triangle are a, b, and c, then $20a = 15b = 12c =$ twice the area of triangle. Dividing by 60, $\frac{a}{3} = \frac{b}{4} = \frac{c}{5}$. Thus, $a{:}b{:}c = 3{:}4{:}5$, and the triangle is a right triangle. Thus, two of the sides of the triangle must be altitudes—the sides with lengths 15 and 20. The area of this triangle is $\boxed{150}$.

Method II: Since $A = \frac{bh}{2}$, $b = \frac{2A}{h}$. The sides are $\frac{A}{6}$, $\frac{2A}{15}$, and $\frac{A}{10}$. The perimeter is $\frac{2A}{5}$, and $s = $ the semiperimeter $= \frac{A}{5}$. By Hero's Formula for the area A of a triangle with sides a, b, and c and with semiperimeter s, $A = \sqrt{s(s-a)(s-b)(s-c)}$. This area equals $\sqrt{(A/5)(A/5 - A/6)(A/5 - 2A/15)(A/5 - A/10)}$. Thus, $A^2 = \frac{A}{5} \times \frac{A}{30} \times \frac{A}{15} \times \frac{A}{10}$, so $1 = \frac{A^2}{150}$ and $A = 150$.

[**NOTE:** It is possible to express the area A of a triangle whose altitudes are h_a, h_b, h_c. This formula is:

$$\frac{1}{A^2} = \left(\frac{1}{h_a} + \frac{1}{h_b} + \frac{1}{h_c}\right)\left(\frac{1}{h_b} + \frac{1}{h_c} - \frac{1}{h_a}\right)\left(\frac{1}{h_a} + \frac{1}{h_c} - \frac{1}{h_b}\right)\left(\frac{1}{h_a} + \frac{1}{h_b} - \frac{1}{h_c}\right).$$

Problem 6-1

Since $\frac{1}{9}+\frac{3}{9}+\frac{5}{9} = 1$ and $\frac{1}{9}+\frac{3}{9} = \frac{4}{9}$, the given equation is equivalent to $1 = \frac{2}{3}+\sqrt{\frac{x}{9}}$, so $x = \boxed{1}$.

Problem 6-2

Since the diagonal d of the rectangle satisfies $d^2 = 6^2+8^2$, $d = 10$. Thus, a diameter of the circle is 10 and the square's area $= \frac{d^2}{2} = \boxed{50}$.

Problem 6-3

Rearranging and factoring, we get $0 = x^{1983}(x^2-1) - x^{1982}(x^2-1) = (x^2-1)(x^{1983}-x^{1982}) = (x-1)(x+1)(x^{1982})(x-1) = (x-1)^2(x+1)(x^{1982})$. Solving this equation, $x = \boxed{-1, 0, 1}$.

Problem 6-4

Method I: Since $999\,999\,999 = (10^9-1)^2 = 10^{18}-2(10)^9+1 = (10^9)(999\,999\,998)+1 = 999\,999\,999\,000\,000\,001$, the number of 9's is $\boxed{8}$.

Method II: Since $n^2 = (n-1)(n+1)+1$, we can write $(999\,999\,999)^2$ as $(999\,999\,998)(10^9)+1$, which equals $999\,999\,998\,000\,000\,001$, which has 8 nine's.

Problem 6-5

Instead of stopping play, continue to unhide all the spaces. It is now becomes clear that there are only 3 key spaces, and the order in which they are unhidden is all that matters. If the X is the last of these that is unhidden, the game has been won; if not, it's a loss. The probability of a win is thus $\boxed{\frac{1}{3}}$.

Problem 6-6

Method I: Rearranging, and then factoring, we get
$x^4(x + 1) + x^2(x + 1) + (x + 1)$
$= (x + 1)[x^4 + x^2 + 1]$
$= (x + 1)[(x^4 + 2x^2 +1) - (x^2)]$
$= (x + 1)[(x^2 + 1)^2 - (x)^2]$
$= (x + 1)[(x^2 + 1 + x)(x^2 + 1 - x)]$
$= \boxed{(x + 1)(x^2 + x + 1)(x^2 - x - 1)}$.

Method II: The given expression is representable as
$\frac{x^6 - 1}{x - 1} = \frac{(x^3 - 1)(x^3 + 1)}{x - 1} = (x^2+x+1)(x+1)(x^2-x+1)$.

Method III: Rearranging and factoring, we will get
$x(x^4+x^2+1)+(x^4+x^2+1) = (x+1)(x^4+x^2+1)$. Now, continuing as shown above in Method I, we get the answer, $(x+1)(x^2+x+1)(x^2-x+1)$.

Method IV: $(x^5+x^4+x^3)+(x^2+x+1) = x^3(x^2+x+1) + (x^2+x+1) = (x^2+x+1)(x^3+1) = (x^2+x+1)(x+1) \times (x^2-x+1)$.

Method V: Group as $x^2(x^3+1)+x(x^3+1)+(x^3+1)$, then continue as in Method IV.

Contests written and compiled by Steven R. Conrad & Daniel Flegler   Mathematics Leagues Inc., © 1985

Problem 1-1

Let r = the length of a radius of one circle. Since $AD = 6r$, $r = 4$, and the area of one circle is $\boxed{16\pi}$.

Problem 1-2

Method I: Rewrite the equation as $(2^2-1^2)+(4^2-3^2)+(6^2-5^2)+(8^2-7^2) = x^2$. Factoring, this can be rewritten as $(2+1)(2-1)+(4+3)(4-3)+(6+5)(6-5)+(8+7)(8-7) = x^2$. Thus, $(2+1)+(4+3)+(6+5)+(8+7) = x^2$, or $1+2+3+4+5+6+7+8 = 36 = x^2$ and $x = \boxed{\pm 6}$.

Method II: By direct computation, $4+16+36+64 = 1+9+25+49+x^2$ and $36 = x^2$.

Problem 1-3

Method I: Since $x^2-y^2 = 100$, it follows that $(x+y)(x-y) = 100$. Since $x+y = 100$, $x-y = 1$. Solving simultaneously, $(x,y) = \boxed{\left(\frac{101}{2}, \frac{99}{2}\right)}$.

Method II: Solve the linear equation for x and substitute the result into the quadratic equation. The result is $(100-y)^2-y^2 = 100$. Simplifying, $200y = 9900$, so $(x,y) = \left(\frac{101}{2}, \frac{99}{2}\right)$.

Problem 1-4

The left side of the given equation is equivalent to $\frac{4^9}{(4^3)^2} = \frac{4^9}{4^6} = 4^3$, from which $x = \boxed{1}$.

Problem 1-5

Let Smith's average be $\frac{h}{b}$, where h is the number of hits and b the number of "at bats." Since $\frac{h}{b} = .300$, the smallest possible values of h and b are 3 and 10 respectively. Let c be the number of "at bats" in the game. Then $\frac{3}{10+c} = .200$ and $c = \boxed{5}$.

Problem 1-6

Method I: Let's stop concentrating on N and let's think about $7N$ instead. (To get N, divide by 7.) We want $7N$ to be the largest 100-digit multiple of 7. Thus, $7N \leq 999\ldots999$; and N is the largest integer less than or equal to $(999\ldots999) \div 7$. By long division, $N = 142857142857\ldots$, a pattern whose 50th digit is $\boxed{4}$.

Method II: If $10^{100}-7 \leq 7N < 10^{100}$, then $N = [10^{100} \div 7] = 142857\ldots$.

Contests written and compiled by Steven R. Conrad & Daniel Flegler   Mathematics Leagues Inc., © 1985

Problem 2-1

The left side factors into $(1985^2)(1+1985)$. Therefore, $k = \boxed{1985^2 \text{ or } 3\,940\,225}$.

Problem 2-2

We are given $a^2+b^2+c^2 = 200$. In a right triangle, $a^2+b^2 = c^2$, so $c^2+c^2 = 200$, and $c = \boxed{10}$.

Problem 2-3

Method I: For a, b, and c to be minimized, let $3a = 4b = 5c = 60$, the least common multiple of 3, 4, 5. Then, $a = 20$, $b = 15$, $c = 12$, and $a+b+c = \boxed{47}$.

Method II: $a+b+c = a+\frac{3a}{4}+\frac{4a}{5} = \frac{47a}{20}$. Since $a+b+c$ is a positive integer, it follows that a is a multiple of 20. The smallest possible value of a is 20, and $a+b+c = 47$.

Problem 2-4

Since $1000^2 = 1\,000\,000$, we must evaluate 1001^2-999^2. Factoring, $1001^2-999^2 = (1001+999)(1001-999) = (2000)(2) = \boxed{4000}$.

Problem 2-5

Method I: Consider the contrapositive of the test sentence: Whenever there is an odd number on one side of the card, there is a consonant on the other side of the card. Since the test sentence and its contrapositive are logically equivalent, we need only turn over $\boxed{A \text{ \& } 3 \ \textbf{or} \ \text{first \& last}}$.

Method II: You need turn over only two cards: the one with the A and the one with the 3. On either card, one could find a vowel paired with an odd number, falsifying the test sentence.

Method III: A is a vowel and F is a consonant (a non-vowel letter); 2 is an even number and 3 is an odd number (a non-even digit). The **statement** "If there is a vowel on one side there is an even number of the other side" suggests turning over the A. The **converse**, "If there is an even number on one side, there's a vowel on the other side" suggests turning over the 2. The **inverse**, "If there is a consonant (non-vowel letter) on one side, there's an odd number (a non-even digit) on the other side" suggests turning over the F. The **contrapositive**, "If there is an odd number (a non-even digit) on one side, there is a consonant (a non-vowel letter) on the other side" suggests turning over the 3. Thus, turn over the A and the 3.

Problem 2-6

Method I: For each burger at Windy's, Burger Queen has 3 additional burgers: 1 with the 1st extra condiment, 1 with the 2nd extra condiment, and 1 with both. Thus, the number of burger types that Windy's has is $\frac{192}{3} = \boxed{64}$.

Method II: Let c be the number of condiments at Windy's. Then, the number of types of burgers at Windy's is 2^c, and the number of types of burgers at Burger Queen's is 2^{c+2}. Since there are 192 more types of burgers at Burger Queen, $2^{c+2} = 2^c+192$. Thus, $2^2(2^c) = 2^c+192$. Solving, $2^c = 64$.

Contests written and compiled by Steven R. Conrad & Daniel Flegler   Mathematics Leagues Inc., © 1985

Problem 3-1

Since $x\% = \frac{x}{100}$, $x\%$ of $x\%$ of $x\%$ of $1\,000\,000 = (\frac{x}{100})^3(1\,000\,000) = (\frac{x^3}{1\,000\,000})(1\,000\,000) = \boxed{x^3}$.

Problem 3-2

Method I: By the triangle inequality, x must be less than 7; and, by the conditions of the problem, x must be 5 or more. Therefore, $x = 5$ or $x = 6$. When $x = 5$, the triangle is a right triangle, so x must equal $\boxed{6}$.

Method II: In a triangle whose longest side is c and whose other sides are a and b, if $c^2 > a^2 + b^2$, the angle opposite side c will be obtuse. A triangle with two sides of 3 and 4 will thus be obtuse when $x = 2$ or $x = 6$; so $x = 6$.

Problem 3-3

For each value of n which is a solution of the inequality, there is also a solution $-n$. For each such pair the average is 0, and the average of all solutions is also $\boxed{0}$.

Problem 3-4

Method I: The region between the two squares is composed of four 1 by x rectangles and four 1 by 1 squares. Since the area of this region is 20, $4 + 4x = 20$, and $x = 4$. Thus the area of the inner square, in cm^2, is $(x)(x) = x^2 = 4^2 = \boxed{16}$.

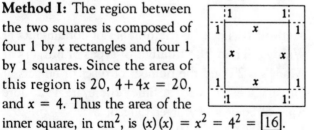

Method II: There's only one way to draw a **border** of 20 squares around a square: put four unit squares in the corners and four additional unit squares on each side. This arrangement can serve as the border only for a 4×4 square whose area is 16.

Problem 3-5

Method I: $4x^3 + 6x^2 + 4x + 1 = 4x^3 + 2x^2 + 4x^2 + 4x + 1 = 2x^2(2x+1) + (2x+1)^2 = \boxed{(2x+1)(2x^2+2x+1)}$.

Method II: Adding and subtracting x^4, $x^4 + 4x^3 + 6x^2 + 4x + 1 - x = (x+1)^4 - x^4 = [(x+1)^2 - x^2][(x+1)^2 + x^2] = (2x+1)(2x^2+2x+1)$.

Method III: Using the rational roots theorem and the factor theorem, a rational root of $4x^2 + 6x^2 + 4x + 1 = 0$ is found to be $-\frac{1}{2}$, so $(2x+1)$ is a factor of the given expression. The other factor can be found by division.

Problem 3-6

Method I: Consider $x^4 + x^2 + (kx + 64) = 0$ as a quadratic in x^2. By the quadratic formula, $x^2 = \frac{1}{2}(-1 \pm D)$, where D^2 is the discriminant of the quadratic. Then, $a = -b = \sqrt{\frac{1}{2}(-1+D)}$ and $c = -d = \sqrt{\frac{1}{2}(-1-D)}$. Now, $a^2 + b^2 + c^2 + d^2 = \frac{1}{2}(-1+D) + \frac{1}{2}(-1+D) + \frac{1}{2}(-1-D) + \frac{1}{2}(-1-D) = \boxed{-2}$.

Method II: Since a, b, c, and d are different numbers, they must be the four solutions of $x^4 + x^2 + kx + 64 = 0$. In a fourth-degree equation whose cubic term is missing, the sum of the roots is 0. Therefore, $a+b+c+d = 0$. Further, by the relationship between the roots and the coefficients, $ab+ac+ad+bc+bd+cd = 1$. Thus, $(a+b+c+d)^2 = 0^2 = a^2+b^2+c^2+d^2 + 2(ab+ac+ad+bc+bd+cd) = a^2+b^2+c^2+d^2+2$, so $a^2+b^2+c^2+d^2 = -2$.

Contests written and compiled by Steven R. Conrad & Daniel Flegler   Mathematics Leagues Inc., © 1985

Problem 4-1

Since $3^2+4^2+12^2 = 13^2$ and $3^2+4^2 = 5^2$, it follows that $13 = 5+x$. Solving, $x = \boxed{8}$.

Problem 4-2

Since 1986 is an even exponent, x^x must equal –1 or 1. Thus, the two possible values of x are $\boxed{-1 \text{ or } 1}$.

Problem 4-3

The value of N is greatest when N has a 9 as its left-most digit and when the other 3 digits are in decreasing order, left to right. Now use trial and error: 9421 is not divisible by 4, but the next largest possibility is, so the answer is $\boxed{9412}$.

Problem 4-4

In the diagram at the right, the probability that a point interior to the outer circle is in region II is proportional to the area of region II. Thus, the probability is $\frac{area\ II}{area\ I+area\ II} = \frac{3\pi}{4\pi} = \boxed{\frac{3}{4}}$.

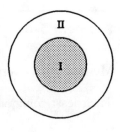

Problem 4-5

Points A and K are the vertices of the acute angles of a right triangle whose legs are 5 and 6. This can be verified by assigning coordinates to the lettered

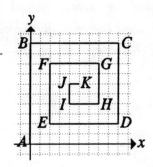

points as indicated in the diagram which accompanies this solution. By the distance formula, the distance from $A(0,0)$ to $K(5,6)$ is $\boxed{\sqrt{61}}$.

Problem 4-6

Method I: Since x and y are positive integers with $x \leq 31$ and $y \leq 44$, there are $31 \times 44 = 1364$ pairings. Roughly one-third of these will be divisible by 3, so the answer is approximately $\boxed{455}$.

Method II: Let's compute the exact number of solutions. *If* we allowed y to have any value from 1 through 45 inclusive, then for each value of x there would be $45/3 = 15$ values of y. The total number of acceptable values would then be $31 \times 15 = 465$. But, y cannot equal 45, and for $y = 45$, we have counted 10 values of x (namely 3, 6, . . . , 30), so the actual answer must be $465 - 10 = 455$.

Method III: Since $x^2 < 1000$, and $y^2 < 2000$, we see that $x \leq 31$ and $y \leq 44$. There are 3 different cases to consider:

Case I: $x \equiv 0 \pmod 3$ and $y \equiv 0 \pmod 3$.
If $x \in \{3,6,\dots,30\}$ and $y \in \{3,6,\dots,42\}$, there are a total of $10 \times 14 = 140$ cases.

Case II: $x \equiv 1 \pmod 3$ and $y \equiv 2 \pmod 3$.
If $x \in \{1,4,\dots,31\}$ and $y \in \{2,5,\dots,44\}$, there are a total of $11 \times 15 = 165$ cases.

Case III: $x \equiv 2 \pmod 3$ and $y \equiv 1 \pmod 3$.
If $x \in \{2,5,\dots,31\}$ and $y \in \{1,4,\dots,43\}$, there are a total of $10 \times 15 = 150$ cases.

The total is $140 + 165 + 150 = 455$.

Contests written and compiled by Steven R. Conrad & Daniel Flegler   Mathematics Leagues Inc., © 1986

Problem 5-1

That any such number must be divisible by 11 is assured by the test for divisibility by 11. Therefore, the only such prime number is $\boxed{11}$.

Problem 5-2

The length of a side of one square is $2\sqrt{2}$. Therefore, the dimensions of the rectangle are $6\sqrt{2}$ by $8\sqrt{2}$. Thus, a diagonal's length is $\boxed{10\sqrt{2} \text{ or } \sqrt{200}}$.

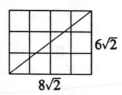

Problem 5-3

The first one, 2222, is clearly less than any of the others. To compare the next two, $22^{22} = (22^2)^{11}$, which is bigger than 222^2. Now, $22^{22} < 32^{22} = (2^5)^{22} = 2^{110} < 2^{222}$; so, of the first four, the largest is 2^{222}. The 5th and last numbers are too small to consider. The contenders are therefore the 4th, 6th, and 7th numbers, and all three are powers of 2. It is evident that the number with the largest exponent is the largest number. Now, of the three exponents, 222, 484, 2^{22}, the last one is clearly the largest, so the largest of the eight numbers is $\boxed{2^{2^{22}}}$.

[**NOTE:** In general, $\left(a^b\right)^c \neq a^{\left(b^c\right)}$, and a^{b^c} is understood to mean $a^{\left(b^c\right)}$. See, for example, p.28 of *The Lore of Large Numbers* by P. J. Davis (New Mathematical Library) or p.25 of *Mathematics and the Imagination*. It should be noted that some calculators do not handle this correctly!]

Problem 5-4

The series on the left side is an arithmetic progression whose $n-1$ terms have a common difference of $\frac{1}{n}$. Since the sum of this series is $\frac{n-1}{2}$, it follows that $\frac{n-1}{2} = 1986$, and $n = \boxed{3973}$.

Problem 5-5

Method I: If $0 < x < 1$, then $0 < x^2 < x$. Thus, $\sin^2 x < \sin x$ and $\sin^2 y < \sin y$, and $\sin^2 x + \sin^2 y = \sin x + \sin y$ if and only if $x = 0°$ or $90°$ and $y = 0°$ or $90°$. So, $(x,y) = \boxed{(0,0), (0,90), (90,0), (90,90)}$.

Method II: By rearranging the terms, we see that $\sin^2 x - \sin x = \sin y - \sin^2 y$; so $\sin x(\sin x - 1) = \sin y(1 - \sin y)$. Since $\sin x$ and $\sin y$ are non-negative, the two sides of this equation have opposite signs, unless both equal 0. The 4 values of (x,y) follow.

Problem 5-6

Method I: Convert the fractions to $\frac{36}{66}, \frac{15}{66}$, and $\frac{8}{66}$. Their least common multiple is $\frac{360}{66} = \boxed{\frac{60}{11}}$.

Method II: The smallest such fraction is the rational number whose numerator is the least common multiple of the numerators and whose denominator is the greatest common divisor of the denominators. The smallest such fraction is $\frac{60}{11}$.

Contests written and compiled by Steven R. Conrad & Daniel Flegler   Mathematics Leagues Inc., © 1986

Problem 6-1

The left side reduces to $x+1$ unless the denominator of the fraction on the left side is 0. Thus, the expressions are not equal when $x = \boxed{1}$.

Problem 6-2

The chords must be perpendicular diameters. By the Pythagorean Theorem, $AC = \boxed{5\sqrt{2}}$.

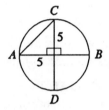

Problem 6-3

The given expression is equivalent to $(8)(2^8) = 2^x$. Thus, $(2^3)(2^8) = 2^x$, or $2^{11} = 2^x$, from which it follows that $x = \boxed{11}$.

Problem 6-4

Let x be my present age and let $n+x$ be Sue's present age. Then, $x = x+2n-4$, and therefore $n = \boxed{2}$.

Problem 6-5

Method I: Using the diagram drawn at the right, $m\angle NMD = \text{Arctan}\frac{1}{2} = m\angle DBC$. Therefore, $m\angle NMD + m\angle NBD = m\angle DBC + m\angle NBD = m\angle NBC = \boxed{45 \text{ or } 45°}$.

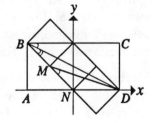

Method II: Coordinatize, using $A(-2,0)$, $B(-2,2)$, $C(2,2)$, $D(2,0)$, $N(0,0)$, and $M(-1,1)$. Let $m\angle NMD = a$ and $m\angle NBD = b$. Use the distance formula and the law of cosines (or use the auxiliary rectangle from Method I) to find $\cos a = \frac{2\sqrt{5}}{5}$ and $\cos b = \frac{3\sqrt{10}}{10}$. Finally, from $\cos(a+b)$ calculate $a+b$.

Method III: Since $\triangle NBD \sim \triangle NDM$, $m\angle NMD + m\angle NBD = m\angle NMD + m\angle NDM = 180 - 135 = 45$.

Problem 6-6

Method I: By the change of base theorem, $\log_x y = \frac{\log_b y}{\log_b x}$, for any suitable base b. The original equation becomes $\frac{\log a}{\log 3} + \frac{\log b}{\log 27} = c$; thus, $\frac{\log a}{\log 3} + \frac{\log b}{3\log 3} = c$. Adding, $\frac{3\log a + \log b}{3\log 3} = \frac{\log a^3 b}{\log 27} = \log_{27} a^3 b = c$. Since $a^3 b = 9$, $\log_{27} 9 = c$. Therefore, $c = \boxed{\frac{2}{3}}$.

Method II: Since $a^3 b = 9$, $a = \left(\frac{9}{b}\right)^{\frac{1}{3}}$. Rewriting the original equation, we find that $\log_3 a + \log_3 b^{\frac{1}{3}} = \log_3 a + \frac{1}{3}\log_3 b = \log_3\left(\frac{9}{b}\right)^{\frac{1}{3}} + \frac{1}{3}\log_3 b = \frac{1}{3}\left(\log_3\frac{9}{b} + \log_3 b\right) = \frac{1}{3}\log_3\left(\frac{9}{b}\cdot b\right) = c$. From this, $\log_3 3^2 = 3c$, so $2 = 3c$, and $c = \frac{2}{3}$.

[**NOTE:** We included the information that $ab^3 = 1986$ because we enjoy including the year in one problem on every contest, and because it is educationally valuable to discriminate between pertinent and non-pertinent data. The ability to make such distinctions comes slowly. We thought we'd help!]

Contests written and compiled by Steven R. Conrad & Daniel Flegler   Mathematics Leagues Inc., © 1986

Problem 1-1

Method I: Every factor $n \leq 5$ can be paired with the factor $m = \frac{30}{n}$ so that $mn = 30$ in each pair. Thus, the product of all 8 factors is $30^4 = (1 \times 30) \times (2 \times 15) \times (3 \times 10) \times (5 \times 6)$, so $k = \boxed{4}$.

Method II: By direct computation, the 8 factors of 30 are 1, 2, 3, 5, 6, 10, 15, 30. Their product is 30^4.

Problem 1-2

Method I: Since AG = CG and EG = FG, $\triangle AEG \cong \triangle CFG$. Thus, AE = 4, AB = 7, and the square's area is $\boxed{49}$.

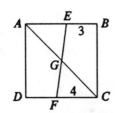

Method II: By symmetry, $\overline{EF}$ goes through the center of the square, so quadrilaterals AEFD and CFEB are $\cong$. The solution then follows that of Method I.

Problem 1-3

Method I: $x^2 - 5x - 6 = (x+1)(x-6)$, so $x^2 + px + q = (x+2)(x-5)$ and $p = \boxed{-3}$.

Method II: $-p$ = new root sum; $p = -3$.

Problem 1-4

Method I: There are at most 26 people with a 1st initial of A and dissimilar 2nd initials. A like statement holds for any 1st initial. Thus, there can be at most 26^2 people none of whom share the same 2 initials. Since 1 more person forces a duplication, the maximum population is $26^2 + 1$ or $\boxed{677}$.

Method II: The number 26^2 follows from *The Fundamental Principle of Counting* (also known as the Multiplication Principle): If a 1st task can be done in A ways, and a 2nd in B ways, there are AB ways to do them in the order 1st followed by 2nd. That 1 more

person forces at least 1 duplication follows from *The Pigeonhole Principle*: More pigeons than pigeonholes forces some pigeonhole to contain at least 2 pigeons.

Problem 1-5

Method I: This continuous, closed curve does not cross itself, so Jordan was either inside or outside the curve after painting. If inside, he'd need an *odd* number of crossings to get outside. He got outside after an *even* number of crossings, so he was already outside when he finished painting! The number of crossings *required* to leave was $\boxed{0 \text{ or none}}$.

Method II: By the *Jordan Curve Theorem*, a simple closed planar curve determines 2 regions, an inside and an outside; the curve is their common boundary.

Problem 1-6

Method I: Solving for a, $a = \frac{b+c-bc}{b+c-bc-1}$, whose numerator and denominator are consecutive integers. Since a is an integer, this occurs only if $a = \frac{0}{-1}$ or $\frac{2}{1}$, so $a = 0$ or 2. Solving for b, and then for c, we get $b = 0$ or 2; and, also, $c = 0$ or 2. If $a = 0$ and $b = 0$, $c = 0$; if $a = 2$ and $b = 0$, $c = 2$; if $a = 2$ and $b = 0$, $c = 2$; if $a = 2$ and $b = 2$, $c = 0$. Therefore, the four solutions are $\boxed{(0,0,0), (2,2,0), (2,0,2), (0,2,2)}$.

Method II: Factoring seems promising. The term abc suggests 3 factors; and a, b, and c suggest each factor contains 1 as a term. Adding 1 to both sides and rearranging, $1 + ab + ac + bc - a - b - c - abc = 1$. Therefore, $(1-a)(1-b)(1-c) = 1$. Since the factors on the left are all integral, either each is 1, or one is 1 while the other two are -1. The four solutions now follow.

Method III: Clearly, $(x-a)(x-b)(x-c) = x^3 - (a+b+c)x^2 + (ab+ac+bc)x - abc$ for all x. When $x = 1$, we get $(1-a)(1-b)(1-c) = 1 - a - b - c + ab + ac + bc - abc$; so, from the given, $(1-a)(1-b)(1-c) = 1$, as above, in **II**.

Contests written and compiled by Steven R. Conrad & Daniel Flegler   Mathematics Leagues Inc., © 1986

Problem 2-1

Many pairs display this particular property, such as $\frac{3}{4}$ and $\frac{4}{3}$, or 25 and $\frac{1}{25}$. Let's prove these positive numbers are reciprocals by showing that their product is always 1. Since $x+y = \frac{1}{x}+\frac{1}{y}$, $x+y = \frac{x+y}{xy}$ and since $x+y \neq 0$, it follows that $xy = \boxed{1}$.

Problem 2-2

Since $x^2-9 = (x+3)(x-3)$, either $x+3 = \pm 1$ or $(x-3) = \pm 1$. Thus, the four values of x, each of which yields a prime, are $\boxed{\pm 2, \pm 4}$.

Problem 2-3

Since $66^{1986} = 6^{1986} \times 11^{1986} = 6^2 \times 6^{1984} \times 11^{1986}$, and since 6^2 has 12 as a factor, 6 must be divisible by 12, so the remainder is $\boxed{0}$.

Problem 2-4

The 2nd day it grew $\frac{1}{2}(100m) = 50m$. The 3rd day it grew $\frac{1}{3}(150m) = 50m$. The 4th day it grew $\frac{1}{4}(200m) = 50m$. In fact, *every day* (except for the 1st day), it grew 50m. After the 1st day, it grew 4900m more, which took 98 more days, for a total of $\boxed{99 \text{ days}}$.

Problem 2-5

Method I: If $m\angle BOC = x$, $m\angle AOB = m\angle DOC = 90-x$. Adding these angles together, $m\angle AOD = 180-x = 4(m\angle BOC) = 4x$ and $x = 36$. Therefore, $m\angle AOD = 4x = \boxed{144°}$.

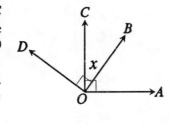

Method II: Adjacent to $\angle AOD$, place an angle congruent to $\angle BOC$, to form a 180° angle. Then, $180 = x+4x = 5x$, so $x = 36$ and $m\angle AOD = 4x = 144°$.

Method III: Get the result of Method II by rotating $\angle DOB$ counter-clockwise about O until $\overline{OB}$ and $\overline{OC}$ coincide.

Method IV: Let $m\angle BOC = x$ and $m\angle AOD = 4x$. By congruence, $m\angle AOB = m\angle COD = 1\frac{1}{2}x$. Since $m\angle AOC = 90° = 2\frac{1}{2}x$, $4x = 144°$.

Method V: Let $m\angle BOC = x$, $m\angle AOB = y$, and $m\angle COD = z$. Then, $x+y = 90$, $x+z = 90$, and $x+y+z = 4x$. Now, solve this system.

Method VI: Let $m\angle DOC = d$, making $m\angle AOD = 90+d$ and $m\angle BOC = 90-d$. Then, $90+d = 4(90-d)$. Solving, $d = 54$, and $90+d = 144$.

Problem 2-6

Method I: Let $a = \sqrt[3]{20 + 14\sqrt{2}}$, $b = \sqrt[3]{20 - 14\sqrt{2}}$. Then $a^3+b^3 = 20 + 14\sqrt{2} + 20 - 14\sqrt{2} = 40$, and $ab = \left(\sqrt[3]{20 + 14\sqrt{2}}\right)\left(\sqrt[3]{20 - 14\sqrt{2}}\right) = \sqrt[3]{400 - 392} = 2$. But $x^3 = (a+b)^3 = a^3 + 3a^2b + 3ab^2 + b^3 = a^3 + b^3 + 3ab(a+b)$. Since $(a+b) = x$, $x^3 = a^3 + b^3 + 3abx$ or $x^3 = 40 + 3(2)x$, so $x^3 - 6x = \boxed{40}$.

Method II: A quick solution is possible if you happen to know that $(2 \pm \sqrt{2})^3 = 20 \pm 14\sqrt{2}$. Knowing this, it is easy to see that $x = 4$ and $x^3 - 6x = 40$.

Contests written and compiled by Steven R. Conrad & Daniel Flegler   Mathematics Leagues Inc., © 1986

Problem 3-1

If the car were blue, it would have to be both a Chevrolet and a Ford, so the car is black. From Lee, it is a Dodge, so it's a $\boxed{\text{black Dodge}}$.

Problem 3-2

Factoring, $(x+1987)(x-1) = 0$, so the 2 values of x are $\boxed{-1987, 1}$.

Problem 3-3

Method I: When 10 numbers average 63, their sum is 10×63 or 630. The 6 numbers averaging 57 have a sum of 342, so the sum of the remaining 4 numbers must be $630 - 342 = 288$; and the average of these 4 numbers is $288 \div 4 = \boxed{72}$.

Method II: The 6 averaging 57 have an average "loss" of $63-57 = 6$ and a total "loss" of $6 \times 6 = 36$. To compensate, the 4 others must gain an average of $36 \div 4 = 9$, so their average is $63+9 = 72$.

Problem 3-4

Since $3^x(3^2) < 3^x+2$, $9(3^x) < 3^x+2$. Subtract 3^x from both sides to get $8(3^x) < 2$, so $3^x < \frac{1}{4}$, and the largest integral value of x is $\boxed{-2}$.

Problem 3-5

Draw radius $\overline{OB}$. In right triangle ODB, $OB = 2$ and $OD = 1$, so $m\angle DOB = 60°$, from which $m\angle AOB = 30°$. Since $\triangle AOB$ is isosceles, $m\angle BAO = \boxed{75°}$.

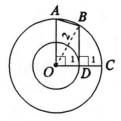

[**NOTE:** Since Arc tan $(2+\sqrt{3}) = 75°$, another acceptable answer is Arc tan $(2+\sqrt{3})$.]

Problem 3-6

Method I: At the point when the 1st satellite finished x orbits, the 2nd satellite was 20 orbits "ahead" of the 3rd. When the second completed an additional 80 orbits, it was 25 orbits "ahead" of the 3rd. For each 80 orbits the 2nd traveled, it "gained" 5 orbits on the 3rd. When the 2nd completed x orbits, it was 25 orbits ahead of the 3rd, so $x = 5(80) = \boxed{400}$.

Method II: When the 1st completed x orbits, the 2nd completed $x-80$ and the 3rd completed $x-100$. When the 2nd completed x orbits, the 3rd completed $x-25$. For any 2 satellites, the ratio of orbits traveled is a constant, so $\frac{x-80}{x-100} = \frac{x}{x-25}$, and $x = 400$.

Contests written and compiled by Steven R. Conrad & Daniel Flegler   Mathematics Leagues Inc., © 1987

Problem 4-1

Since $(\frac{2}{x} - \frac{x}{2})^2 = 0$, $\frac{2}{x} = \frac{x}{2}$. Solving, $x^2 = 4$, and $(x^2)^3 = x^6 = \boxed{64}$.

Problem 4-2

From the statement of the problem, $\left(\frac{x}{100}\right)\left(\frac{x}{100}\right) = \frac{x}{100}$, so $\frac{x}{100}\left(\frac{x}{100} - 1\right) = 0$. Therefore, $\frac{x}{100} = 0$, or $\frac{x}{100} - 1 = 0$. Solving, $x = \boxed{0, 100}$.

Problem 4-3

Let N be the midpoint of $\overline{BC}$. Draw $\overline{MN}$. Then draw, to M, a radius of the semicircle. Since $AB = 7$ and the radius is 3, $MN = 4$. But $BN = NC = 3$, so triangles BNM and CNM are 3–4–5 triangles. Finally, the perimeter of triangle MBC is $5+5+6 = \boxed{16}$.

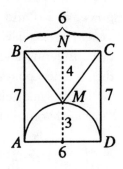

Problem 4-4

This problem generalizes very easily, so let's compute the sum of *any* four consecutive powers of i. When i is raised to any positive integral power, the result must be i, -1, $-i$, or 1. In every set of four consecutive powers of i, each power equals a different one of these 4 results. Thus, the sum equals $i-1-i+1 = \boxed{0}$.

Problem 4-5

Method I: If $9N = 11 \ldots 1$, then $N = (11 \ldots 11) \div 9$. Therefore, divide a string of 1's by 9 until the remainder is 0—and the quotient is $\boxed{12\,345\,679}$.

Method II: Since the string of 1's is divisible by 9, the test for divisibility by 9 assures us that $9N$ has 9 1's. Finally, $(111\,111\,111) \div 9 = 12\,345\,679$.

Problem 4-6

In the chart below, "# right" represents the least number of questions a student must answer correctly to qualify for the next test—the AIME.

#answered	# right	# wrong	# blank	score
14	14	0	16	102
15	14	1	15	100
16	15	1	14	103
17	15	2	13	101
18	16	2	12	104
19	16	3	11	102
20	16	4	10	100
21	17	4	9	103
22	17	5	8	101
23	18	5	7	104
24	18	6	6	102
25	18	7	5	100
26	19	7	4	103
27	19	8	3	101
28	20	8	2	104
29	20	9	1	102
30	20	10	0	100

As seen in this chart, 23 questions answered, with 16 right, 7 wrong, or 17 right, 6 wrong, doesn't qualify—but answering 2 more questions could raise the score to 18 right, 7 wrong and thus qualify. (A student correctly answering 18 of 23 questions doesn't jeopardize qualification by answering 2 more questions.) From the chart, it is observed that N, $N+1$, and $N+2$ require the same *minimum* number correct for $N = \boxed{18, 23, 28}$.

Contests written and compiled by Steven R. Conrad & Daniel Flegler   Mathematics Leagues Inc., © 1987

Problem 5-1

Method I: $100 = 64+32+4 = 2^6+2^5+2^2$ and $6+5+2 = \boxed{13}$.

Method II: The base two representation of one hundred is 1100100, from which the solution continues as above. The uniqueness of representation in any base assures us there's only one answer.

Method III: Since $10 = 2^3+2$, $10^2 = (2^3+2)^2 = (2^3)^2+2(2^3)(2)+2^2$, and continue as in Method I.

Problem 5-2

For a round peg in a square hole, the ratio of the cross-sectional area of the peg to the cross-sectional area of the hole is $\frac{\pi r^2}{4r^2} = \frac{\pi}{4}$. For a square peg in a round hole, the ratio of areas is $\frac{2r^2}{\pi r^2} = \frac{2}{\pi}$. The first ratio exceeds $\frac{3}{4}$ and the second is less than $\frac{2}{3}$. The better fit is $\boxed{\text{a round peg in a square hole}}$.

Problem 5-3

Since all the exponents are even, if x is a solution, $-x$ is also a solution, so the other root is $\boxed{-2}$.

[NOTE: Descartes' Rule of Signs can be used to prove that there are no other real roots.]

Problem 5-4

Method I: If V is the number of votes cast, then $\frac{V-1}{V} > 94\%$, so $1 - \frac{1}{V} > 94\%$, or $\frac{1}{V} < \frac{3}{50}$. Thus, $3V > 50$, so the least integral V is $\boxed{17}$.

Method II: The answer is less than or equal to 20, since $\frac{19}{20}$ is 95%. By trial and error, the answer is 17.

Problem 5-5

[*All logs are base 10.*] If n is an integer, the number of digits in n is 1 more than the characteristic of $\log n$. Since $1987 \times (\log 3) = 1987 \times 0.47712 = 948.03744$, and $1987 \times (\log 2) = 1987 \times 0.30103 = 598.14661$, $d = 949 - 599 = \boxed{350}$.

Problem 5-6

Method I: The sum of two powers of 2 is a third power of 2 if and only if the powers of 2 are the same. For example, $2^2+2^2 = 2^3$. It's easy to see this by considering addition of two numbers in base 2: there's a new power of 2 only when each addend has a 1 in the same column (or when a carry creates the same situation). Let $a^3 = (2^x)^3$ and $b^4 = (2^y)^4$. If $a^3 = b^4$, then $3x = 4y$, so y is a multiple of 3. Since $a^3 + b^4 = 2b^4 = 2(2^y)^4 = 2^{4y+1} = c^5$, we see that $4y+1$ is a multiple of 5. Thus, $y = 6$ and $x = 8$. The original equation is $(2^8)^3+(2^6)^4 = (2^5)^5$, and $a+b+c = 2^8+2^6+2^5 = 256+64+32 = \boxed{352}$.

Method II: Let $a = 2^x$, $b = 2^y$, $c = 2^z$. Then, $2^{3x}+2^{4y} = 2^{5z}$. Dividing by 2^{5z}, we get $2^{3x-5z} + 2^{4y-5z} = 1$. Two powers of 2 add up to 1 if and only if each is $\frac{1}{2}$. Thus, $3x - 5z = -1$ and $4y - 5z = -1$, from which $(x,y,z) = (8,6,5)$. The solution then continues as in Method I.

Contests written and compiled by Steven R. Conrad & Daniel Flegler — Mathematics Leagues Inc., © 1987

Problem 6-1

If $(x-a)^2 = (x+a)^2$, then $x^2-2ax+a^2 = x^2+2ax+a^2$. Thus, $4ax = 0$. For this equation to be valid for all values of x, $a = \boxed{0}$.

Problem 6-2

$x^{32} = (x^{64})^{\frac{1}{2}} = (64)^{\frac{1}{2}} = \boxed{8}$.

Problem 6-3

Method I: Surround the quadrilateral with a rectangle whose vertices are $O(0,0)$, $A(0,3)$, $E(5,3)$, and $D(5,0)$, and whose area is $3 \times 5 = 15$. The areas of right triangles OAD and CBE are, respectively, $7\frac{1}{2}$ and 1. The quadrilateral's area is $15 - 7\frac{1}{2} - 1 = \boxed{6\frac{1}{2}}$.

Method II: Draw $\overline{BD}$, creating $\triangle ABD$ and $\triangle BCD$. For the area of $\triangle ABD$, use base $\overline{AB}$ and altitude $\overline{DE}$. For $\triangle BCD$, use base $\overline{CD}$ and altitude $\overline{BE}$. Add the results to get the area of $ABCD$.

Problem 6-4

Keith tossed 1 more coin than Brian, so he must have tossed either more heads or more tails, *but not both*. Each outcome is equally likely, so each probability is $\boxed{\frac{1}{2} \text{ or } 50\% \text{ or } 0.5}$.

[**NOTE 1:** The *odds* that Keith gets more heads than Brian are 1 to 1. It's easy to calculate probability when given odds. This question asked for the probability, not the odds, so a student who gives the odds, has *not* correctly answered the question asked.]

[**NOTE 2:** The probability is ½ whenever Keith tosses 1 more coin than Brian. If he tosses 2 more coins than Brian, the probability would depend on the number of coins Brian tosses. The computation is involved—the answer is *not* ¾.]

Problem 6-5

Method I: There are 10 numbers on the clock, so it takes 6 minutes for the minute hand to move from one number to the next, and 18 minutes to move from the 10 to the 3. Starting at the 3:00 position, the hands will first coincide when the hour hand has moved x minutes and the minute hand $18+x$ minutes. The minute hand moves 10 times as fast as the hour hand, so $10x = 18+x$, $x = 2$, $18+x = 20$, and the time when the two hands coincide is $\boxed{3{:}20}$.

Method II: In x minutes, the minute hand is $x/6$ minutes from the 10, and the hour hand is $3 + x/60$ minutes from the 10. Equating, $x = 20$.

Problem 6-6

Method I: $2 \sin 36° \cos 36° = \sin 72° = \sin 108°$, and $2 \sin 108° \cos 108° = \sin 216° = -\sin 36°$, so we have $\cos 36° \cos 108° = \dfrac{\sin 108°}{2 \sin 36°} \times \dfrac{-\sin 36°}{2 \sin 108°} = \boxed{\dfrac{-1}{4}}$.

Method II: $\cos 36° \cos 108° = (\cos 36°)(-\cos 72°) = \dfrac{(2 \sin 36° \cos 36°)(-\cos 72°)}{2 \sin 36°} = \dfrac{(\sin 72°)(-\cos 72°)}{2 \sin 36°} = \dfrac{-2 \sin 72° \cos 72°}{4 \sin 36°} = \dfrac{-\sin 144°}{4 \sin 36°} = \dfrac{-\sin 36°}{4 \sin 36°} = \dfrac{-1}{4}$.

Method III: $\cos 36° \cos 108° = -\cos 36° \cos 72° = -\sin 54° \sin 18° = \dfrac{-\sin 18° \cos 18° \sin 54° \cos 54°}{4 \cos 18° \cos 54°} = \dfrac{-\sin 36° \sin 108°}{4 \cos 54° \cos 18°} = \dfrac{-\sin 36° \sin 72°}{4 \sin 36° \sin 72°} = \dfrac{-1}{4}$.

Method IV: In the diagram, let $AC = 2$ and let $BC = x$. In $\triangle ADE$, $\cos 36° = \dfrac{1}{x}$. In $\triangle ABF$, $\cos 108° = -\cos 72° = -\dfrac{\frac{1}{2}x}{2} = \dfrac{-x}{4}$, so $\cos 36° \cos 108° = -\frac{1}{4}$.

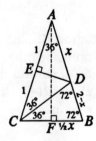

Contests written and compiled by Steven R. Conrad & Daniel Flegler   Mathematics Leagues Inc., © 1987

Problem 1-1

Since $a = -b$, the numerator and denominator are opposites, and the value of their quotient is $\boxed{-1}$.

Problem 1-2

Since the 8 year-old dog would be 56 years old as a human, the age ratio of humans to dogs is 7:1. Thus, if my 42 year-old father were a dog, his age would be $42 \div 7 = \boxed{6}$.

Problem 1-3

Since $x^2 = |x|^2$, the original equation can be written as $|x|^2 + 5|x| - 6 = 0$. So, $(|x|+6)(|x|-1) = 0$, and $|x| = 1$. Therefore, $x = \boxed{-1,1}$.

Problem 1-4

The sum of the lengths of any two sides of a triangle must be greater than the length of the third side. Consequently, the longest side must be less then the sum of the other sides. Starting with the longest side, and writing the other sides in decreasing order, the only possible triples of integers are (7,7,1), (7,6,2), (7,5,3), (7,4,4), (6,6,3), (6,5,4), and (5,5,5). The number of such triangles is $\boxed{7}$.

Problem 1-5

Method I: $a^2 - b^2 = a - b$. Since $a - b \neq 0$, divide both sides by $a-b$ to get $a+b = 1$ or $\boxed{a = -b+1}$.

Method II: Since this is a quadratic equation, there is only one other possibility besides $a = b$; so if we guess well, we'll find the solution. Picking numbers, $3(2) = -2(-3)$. In this case $a = 3$ and $b = -2$, and $a \neq b$. Instead, $a = -b+1$.

Method III: Since $a \neq b$, try $a = b-1$, try $a = -b$, and try $a = -(b-1)$. The last one checks.

Method IV: $a^2 - a + b - b^2 = (a-b)(a-1+b) = 0$, etc.

Method V: Complete the square: $a^2 - a + \frac{1}{4} = b^2 - b + \frac{1}{4}$, so $(a-\frac{1}{2})^2 = (b-\frac{1}{2})^2$. Then, $a - \frac{1}{2} = \pm(b-\frac{1}{2})$, etc.

Method VI: $a^2 - a + (b - b^2) = 0$. By the quadratic formula, $a = \frac{1 \pm \sqrt{1 - 4b + 4b^2}}{2} = \frac{1 \pm (2b-1)}{2}$. Be careful to use only $a = \frac{1 - (2b-1)}{2}$, or you'll get $a = b$.

Method VII: Let $a = b+x$. Substituting into the original equation and simplifying, $x(x+2b+1) = 0$. Since $a \neq b$, $x \neq 0$. Thus, $x = 1-2b$ and $a = 1-b$.

Problem 1-6

Method I: The averages at vertices E, D, and G are the same. Since all have H as a near vertex, it follows that $A+F = F+C = A+C$. Thus, $A = F = C$. From vertex B, they average 3, so each is $\boxed{3}$.

Method II: In each equation, let letters on the right represent values hidden at each vertex. If we triple the number at each vertex, we get the sum of values hidden at the 3 nearest vertices. Thus, we can write:

$$\begin{array}{ll} \text{(for vertex } B\text{):} & 9 = A + C + F \\ \text{(for vertex } D\text{):} & 15 = A + C + H \\ \text{(for vertex } E\text{):} & 15 = A + F + H \end{array}$$

Adding, $39 = 3A + 2C + 2F + 2H$; or $39 = 3A + 2(C+F+H)$. From vertex G, we get $15 = C+F+H$, so it follows that $39 = 3A + 2(15)$, and $A = 3$.

Method III: From Method II we see that the value hidden at A equals the sum of the seen values at B, D, and E, minus twice the value seen at G.

Contests written and compiled by Steven R. Conrad & Daniel Flegler   Mathematics Leagues Inc., © 1987

Problem 2-1

Method I: By trial, the first such n occurs when the sum is 36—and, in that case, $n = \boxed{8}$.

Method II: Let the expression simplify to the integer x. By the formula for the sum of an arithmetic progression, $n(n+1) = 2x^2$. The first square whose double is the product of two consecutive integers is 36, since $8 \times 9 = 2 \times 36 = 72$. Thus, $n = 8$.

Problem 2-2

If x and y are integers with $2x^2 = 3y^2$, there are two possibilities. If $x \neq 0$, then $\frac{2}{3} = \frac{y^2}{x^2} = (\frac{y}{x})^2$. Since $\frac{2}{3}$ is *not* the square of a rational number, $(x,y) = \boxed{(0,0)}$.

Problem 2-3

If the sides of the rectangle are $2x$ and $2y$, the legs of the right triangle are $x\sqrt{2}$ and $y\sqrt{2}$, respectively. The sum of the areas of the 4 triangles is $2x^2+2y^2 = 200$. Finally, each diagonal is $\sqrt{4x^2+4y^2} = \sqrt{400} = \boxed{20}$.

Problem 2-4

If the numbers are $x+1$ and x, and if the difference of their squares is 1987, then $(x+1)^2-x^2 = (x^2+2x+1)-x^2 = 2x+1$. The sum needed $= 2x+1 = \boxed{1987}$.

Problem 2-5

There are four cases. If both expressions are positive, removal of absolute values gives $(x+y)+(x-y) = 2x = 4$, so $x = 2$. If both are negative, $-(x+y)-(x-y) = -2x = 4$, so $x = -2$. If the expressions have opposite signs, the simplification produces $y = 2$ or $y = -2$. The region bounded by segments of these 4 lines is a square of side-length 4 with sides parallel to the axes. The area of this square is $\boxed{16}$.

Problem 2-6

Let $a \leq b \leq c \leq d \leq e$ be the 5 integers. There are 10 ways to sum them 2 at a time: $a+b$, $a+c$, $a+d$, $a+e$, $b+c$, $b+d$, $b+e$, $c+d$, $c+e$, and $d+e$. But only 9 different sums are given. If 2 (or more) of the 5 integers were equal, there would be fewer than 9 sums, so all 5 integers are different.

Method I: Since $d+e$ is the largest sum and $c+e$ is the 2nd largest, $c+d+2e = 2269$. Since $2e$ is even, $c+d$ is odd; so the 3rd largest sum, 1040, cannot be $c+d$ and must be $b+e$. Thus, $c+d = 951$. Hence, $951+2e = 2269$, so $2e = 1318$ and $e = \boxed{659}$.

Method II: There are 3 even and 6 odd sums, so 5 of the numbers *must* be 3 of one parity and 2 of the other. If the numbers of like parity are x, y, and z, their pairwise sums must be even. Thus, $x+y = 794$, $z+z = 1040$, and $y+z = 1072$. Solving, $x = 381$, $y = 413$, and $z = 659$. The other two numbers are 256 and 538, so the largest is 659.

Method III: Since $a+b = 637$ and $a+c = 669$, $c-b = 32$, an even number. But, c is integral only if $c+b$ is even. Thus, $c+b = 794$ (since $b+d$, $b+e$, $c+d$, $c+e$, and $d+e$ exceed $c+b$ and $c = 413$. Since $c+e = 1072$, $e = 659$.

Method IV: Since $a+b = 637$ and $a+c = 669$, $c-b = 32$. Also, $951-919 = 1072-1040 = 32$, so the sum $c+b$, which must be even, is 794, the only sum remaining. Thus, $2c = 826$, and $c = 413$. Since $c+e = 1072$, $e = 659$.

Method V: The total of all 10 possible sums is $4(a+b+c+d+e)$. The total of the given sums is 8194. Division by 4 leaves a remainder of 2, so the repeated sum must also leave a remainder of 2—and it must be 794. Thus, $a+b+c+d+e = (8194 + 794)/4 = 2247$. Since all 5 numbers are distinct, 794 must be the sum of 2 disjoint pairs; so one of the 5 numbers, x, is $2247-794-794 = 659$. Checking with the given sums, this is the largest.

Contests written and compiled by Steven R. Conrad & Daniel Flegler   Mathematics Leagues Inc., © 1987

Problem 3-1

Method I: If $x \neq 0$, dividing by x^{1987} gives us $1 = x$. The other possibility is $x = 0$, so $x = \boxed{0,1}$.

Method II: Since $x^{1988} - x^{1987} = x^{1987}(x-1)$. Therefore, either $x^{1987} = 0$ or $x - 1 = 0$. Solving, either $x = 0$ or $x = 1$.

Problem 3-2

Raising both sides of the equation to the 5th, $x = 4^5$, so $\sqrt{x} = 2^5 = \boxed{32}$.

Problem 3-3

The area of the semicircle is 18π; so its radius is 6, and the base of the rectangle is 12. Since the area of the rectangle is $6\pi + 18\pi = 24\pi$, the width of the rectangle is 2π. Finally, the perimeter $= \boxed{24 + 4\pi}$.

Problem 3-4

Since $(5^{-2})^x (5^3)^{x^2} = (5^3)^x (5^{-2})$, we can equate exponents, getting $-2x + 3x^2 = 3x - 2$ or $3x^2 - 5x + 2 = 0$. Factoring, $(3x-2)(x-1) = 0$. Both solutions check, and they are $x = \boxed{\frac{2}{3}, 1}$.

Problem 3-5

Method I: Let's look at the money that's there at each stage. First, we have \$x. Next year we have $k(\$x)$. The second year we have $k[k(\$x)] > \$2x$, so $k^2 > 2$ and $k > \sqrt{2} = 141.4+\%$. Since the principal is 100%, the least rate of interest must be $\boxed{41.5\%}$.

Method II: Let the rate of interest be r, and let the original principal be P. After the 1st year, the principal becomes $P + rP$. The second year, the principal becomes $(P + rP) + r(P + rP) > 2P$. The question is meaningless unless $P \neq 0$, so we may divide both sides of this inequality by P to get $r^2 + 2r - 1 > 0$. The least positive solution of the inequality is given by $r = \sqrt{2} - 1$, which rounds *up* to $r = 41.5\%$.

Problem 3-6

We'll put the work on the left and explain it on the right.

$$\begin{array}{r} ABCDE \\ \times 4 \\ \hline EDCBA \end{array}$$

Since $4E$ has A as its units' digit A, A is even. On the left, $4A$ (+ a possible carry) = E, a single digit, so A = 2 and E is 8 or 9. On the right, $4E$ has units' digit A = 2, so E = 8.

$$\begin{array}{r} 2BCD8 \\ \times 4 \\ \hline 8DCB2 \end{array}$$

Since $4D+3$ has units' digit B, B is odd. On the left, since $4B$ (+ a possible carry) = D, a single digit, B = 1. Since $4D+3$ has B = 1 as its units' digit, D = 7.

$$\begin{array}{r} 21C78 \\ \times 4 \\ \hline 87C12 \end{array}$$

Since $4C+3$ has units' digit C, C = 9, from which we can conclude that $ABCDE = \boxed{21978}$.

[NOTE: $4(2199 \ldots 9978) = 8799 \ldots 9912.$]

Contests written and compiled by Steven R. Conrad & Daniel Flegler   Mathematics Leagues Inc., © 1988

Problem 4-1

Since vertical angles are congruent, the unshaded sector of the lower left quadrant has the same area as the shaded sector of the upper right quadrant. Thus, the sum of the areas of the shaded regions is equal to the area of a quadrant, and the per cent of the circle it occupies is $\boxed{25, \text{ or } 25\%}$.

Problem 4-2

By inspection, $x = 10$ is a root of the given equation. Since, by *Descartes' Rule of Signs* (or by factoring), there are no other positive roots, the value required is $\boxed{1988}$.

Problem 4-3

The sides of the second triangle must be 10, 14, and 20; and its perimeter will be $10 + 14 + 20 = \boxed{44}$.

Problem 4-4

Method I: Since the right side of the given inequality is non-negative, it follows that $\sin x$ is positive. If we square both sides, we get $\sin^2 x > \frac{1}{2}$, or $\sin x > \frac{\sqrt{2}}{2}$. Hence, the solution is $\boxed{45° < x < 135°}$.

Method II: Since $\sqrt{x^2} = |x|$ and $1 - \sin^2 x = \cos^2 x$, the problem requires us to solve $\sin x > |\cos x|$, $0° < x < 360°$. From the graph, the solution set is $\{x \mid 45° < x < 135°\}$.

Problem 4-5

Method I: In base thirteen, the number 1 million is 290221, meaning there were 2 prizes of \$371 293, 9 prizes of \$28 561, 2 prizes of \$169, 2 prizes of \$13, and 1 prize of \$1. The least possible number of prizes was $\boxed{16}$.

Method II: To have the fewest number of prizes, have as many of the biggest prize as possible before awarding any of the smaller prizes. There can be at most 2 prizes of \$371 293. The other prizes are those detailed in Method I.

Problem 4-6

Rewriting both equations we'll get
$$(x + y)^2 - 3xy = 13 \quad (1),$$
$$\text{and } (x + y) - xy = -5 \quad (2).$$
Tripling (2) and subtracting from (1), we get $(x+y)^2 - 3(x+y) - 28 = 0$, or $(x+y-7)(x+y+4) = 0$. Therefore, $x+y = 7$ or $x+y = -4$. From (2), if $x+y = 7$, then $xy = 12$; if $x+y = -4$, then $xy = 1$. The 4 solutions of these two equation systems are:
$$\boxed{(3,4),(4,3),(-2+\sqrt{3},-2-\sqrt{3}),(-2-\sqrt{3},-2+\sqrt{3})}.$$

Contests written and compiled by Steven R. Conrad & Daniel Flegler   Mathematics Leagues Inc., © 1988

Problem 5-1

The length of a side of the smaller square must be $\frac{1}{4}$, so a side of the larger square is $4(\frac{1}{4}) = 1$ and the perimeter of the large square is $\boxed{4}$.

Problem 5-2

Since $x^2 = 100$, $x = 10$ or -10; and since $x^3 \neq 1000$, $x = -10$. Therefore, $x^5 = \boxed{-10^5 \text{ or } -100\,000}$.

Problem 5-3

Method I: By 12:30, 27 had been consumed, so only 54 remained. By 1 PM, another 18 had been eaten, leaving 36; by 1:30, 12 more were gone, leaving 24; by 2 PM, 8 more were taken, leaving $\boxed{16}$.

Method II: The number of beans that remain form the geometric progression $81(\frac{2}{3})$, $81(\frac{2}{3})^2$, $81(\frac{2}{3})^3$, $81(\frac{2}{3})^4$, a series whose last term is $2^4 = 16$.

Problem 5-4

For any allowable base, we have that $\log 1 + \log 9 + \log 8 + \log 8 = \log(1 \times 9 \times 8 \times 8) = \log(3^2 \times 8^2) = 2\log 24$. Thus, $k = \boxed{24}$.

Problem 5-5

The angle formed by the two tangents drawn from an outside point to a circle is bisected by the line which connects 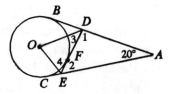 the point to the center. Thus, $\overline{DO}$ and $\overline{EO}$ bisect $\angle BDF$ and $\angle CEF$ respectively. In the diagram below, since $m\angle A = 20$, $m\angle 1 + m\angle 2 = 160$, and the sum of their supplements is 200. But, since $\angle 3$ and $\angle 4$ are together half this measure, the sum of their measures is 100; so, in $\triangle DOE$, $m\angle DOE = \boxed{80}$.

Problem 5-6

Call the roots p and q. It follows that $(p-1) + (q-1) = p+q-2 > 0$, so $\frac{3a}{a+1} - 2 > 0$, $\frac{a-2}{a+1} > 0$. Therefore, $a < -1$ or $a > 2$. Also, $(p-1) + (q-1) = pq - (p+q) + 1 > 0$, so $\frac{2a+1}{a+1} > 0$; and $a < -1$ or $a > -\frac{1}{2}$. Finally, since the discriminant of the original equation must be positive, $9a^2 - 16a(a+1) = -a(7a+16) > 0$; so $-\frac{16}{7} < a < 0$. The final conditions of the third, the fourth, and the fifth sentences will all be satisfied if $\boxed{-\frac{16}{7} < a < -1}$.

Contests written and compiled by Steven R. Conrad & Daniel Flegler   Mathematics Leagues Inc., © 1988

Problem 6-1

When p is a prime, the sum of its factors is $p+1$, so $p+1 = 1988$ and $p = \boxed{1987}$.

Problem 6-2

When we divide x by $x-2$, the result is $1 + \dfrac{2}{x-2}$. Thus, $x-2$ must be a factor of 2. The possibilities are $x-2 = -2, -1, 1,$ or 2. Solving, $x = \boxed{0, 1, 3, 4}$.

Problem 6-3

It's easy enough, by picking values for a, b, c, and d, to guess the answer. Let's prove that this answer is correct. Since all quantities are positive, taking reciprocals reverses the direction of inequality, so $\dfrac{b}{a} > \dfrac{d}{c}$ > 1. Further, since $\dfrac{d}{c} > 1$, $\left(\dfrac{b}{a}\right)\left(\dfrac{d}{c}\right) = \dfrac{bd}{ac} > \dfrac{b}{a}$. The only one not positioned is $\dfrac{b+d}{a+c}$, known as the *mediant* of $\dfrac{b}{a}$ and $\dfrac{d}{c}$. The mediant of two fractions always lies between the two fractions (it doesn't add enough to the larger to keep up with the larger, and it adds enough to the smaller to bypass the smaller). In increasing order, they are $\boxed{1, \dfrac{d}{c}, \dfrac{b+d}{a+c}, \dfrac{b}{a}, \dfrac{bd}{ac}}$.

Problem 6-4

Let n be the number of coins originally in the jar. Since their average value was 16¢, their total value was $(16n)$¢. Since adding a quarter raised the average value to 17¢, we get $\dfrac{16n + 25}{n+1} = 17$. Solving, $n = 8$,

and the total value is $8(16¢) = \$1.28$. This can only occur when there are 3 pennies; so the other 5 coins must be quarters, and the required probability is $\boxed{\dfrac{5}{8}}$.

Problem 6-5

Method I: The area of the triangle is $\frac{1}{2}(36)(\sin x°) = 18\sin x°$, so $18\sin x° + 32\pi = 36\pi$. Solving, $\sin x° = \boxed{\dfrac{2\pi}{9}}$.

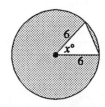

Method II: Let h be the length of an altitude of the triangle, drawn to the radius of the circle. Then, the area of the triangle is $3h$, so $h = \frac{4\pi}{3}$. In the triangle, $\sin x° = \frac{h}{6}$. Now, by substitution, solve for $\sin x°$.

Problem 6-6

Method I: Let $\sqrt{x-1} = t$. Then $x = t^2 + 1$ and $t \geq 0$. The given equation becomes $t+1 + |t-1| = 2t$. This is true if and only if $t \geq 1$. Thus, $\boxed{x \geq 2}$.

Method II: All quantities are positive, so we may square both sides. On the left we get $x + 2\sqrt{x-1} + x - 2\sqrt{x-1} + 2\sqrt{x^2-4(x-1)} = 2x + 2\sqrt{x^2-4x+4}$. On the right side we get $4x - 4$. Thus, $\sqrt{x^2-4x+4} = x-2$. Now, since $\sqrt{x^2-4x+4} = \sqrt{(x-2)^2} = |x-2|$, the prior equation is equivalent to $|x-2| = x-2$. This is true if and only if $x \geq 2$.

[**NOTE:** Is the equation satisfied by $x = 0$, since, if $x = 0$, we get $1+i + (-1+i) = 2$? Is 0 in the domain? Mathematicians require that functions, such as the expression on the left side of the original equation, be treated as the *sum* of two other functions, each of which must be real-valued. Thus, x cannot be 0.]

Contests written and compiled by Steven R. Conrad & Daniel Flegler   Mathematics Leagues Inc., © 1988

Problem 1-1

Method I: The triangle is similar to a 3-4-5 triangle, with ratio of similitude of 111:1. Thus, the length of the hypotenuse is $5(111) = \boxed{555}$.

Method II: By the Pythagorean Theorem, $333^2 + 444^2 = x^2 = 555^2$, so $x = 555$.

Problem 1-2

At each turn, if Ann takes 1, Bob should take 2; and if Ann takes 2, Bob should take 1. If the number of coins Bob leaves is always a multiple of 3, eventually there will be no coins left, and the winner of the game will be $\boxed{\text{Bob}}$.

[**NOTE:** A variation of this strategy is the right approach—no matter how many coins there are initially! For example, if a player could take 1, 2, 3, 4, 5, 6, or 7 coins, and if there were 100 coins at the start, then the first player could guarantee a win by first removing 4 coins and then, in subsequent moves, being sure that the number of coins left in the pile is always a multiple of 8.]

Problem 1-3

The second hand makes 71 rotations and its length is 14 cm., so the total distance it travels $= (71)(2\pi r) = 71(28\pi) = 1988\pi$, from which $k = \boxed{1988}$.

Problem 1-4

Expressing each factor as a simple fraction, the resulting product is $(\frac{1}{2})(\frac{2}{3})(\frac{3}{4}) \times \ldots \times (\frac{97}{98})(\frac{98}{99})(\frac{99}{100})$. The "telescoping" product reduces to $\boxed{\frac{1}{100}}$.

Problem 1-5

Method I: Since the ratio of the distances traveled when the trains pass is 11:4 (the faster train covering the greater distance), the faster train will have taken $\frac{11}{15}$ of the usual time it needs to travel the whole distance. The trains will pass at $(\frac{11}{15})(8$ hrs$)$ past noon, which is 5:52 or $\boxed{5{:}52 \text{ PM}}$.

[**NOTE:** From the perspective of the slower train, the two trains will meet at $(\frac{4}{15})(22$ hrs$)$ past noon = 5:52 PM.]

Method II: If we let d be the distance between New York and Toronto, then the rate of the slower train is $\frac{d}{22}$ while the rate of the faster is $\frac{d}{8}$. If each has traveled t hours when they pass, we can write $(\frac{d}{8})t + (\frac{d}{22})t = d$, since the sum of the distances traveled by the two trains equals the distance between New York and Toronto = d. Solving, $t = \frac{88}{15}$ hours, just as before.

Problem 1-6

Adding the three equations, we get $(2x+2y+2z)(x+y+z) = 288$, from which it follows that $(x+y+z)^2 = 144$, and then $x+y+z = \pm12$. Substitute this back into each of the original equations, and we get $x+y = \pm10$, $y+z = \pm8$, and $x+z = \pm6$. Now subtract these results from the equation $x+y+z = \pm12$ to see that $(x,y,z) = \boxed{(4,6,2), (-4,-6,-2)}$.

Problem 2-1

Expanding, $1988^2 - 2(1988)x + x^2 = x^2$. Solving, $x = \frac{1988}{2}$ (which is really obvious once you think about it) or $x = \boxed{994}$.

Problem 2-2

Trial and error works well. Here is an algebraic approach: We are told that $p = t + 1$ and also that $p = 2(t - 1)$. Solving, $p = 4$ and $t = \boxed{3}$.

Problem 2-3

Method I: We know that $4^4 = 256$, so the left side is 16. The number 16 can be written as an integral power in only 3 ways: 2^4, 4^2, and 16^1. Therefore, $(a,b) = \boxed{(2,4),\ (4,2),\ (16,1)}$.

Method II: Take the square root without first raising to the fourth power. We can do this either by dividing the exponent by 2 (leaving the base alone), and getting (4,2), or by extracting the square root of the base (and not changing the exponent), getting (2,4). From these two, we can get the third answer.

Problem 2-4

Since the ratio of the length of the tangent to the length of a radius of the larger circle is $2:1.5 = 4:3$, and since the tangent is perpendicular to this

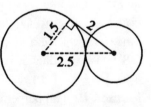

radius, the triangle whose vertices are the two centers and the point of tangency is a 3-4-5 type right triangle with sides of lengths $\frac{3}{2}$, $\frac{4}{2}$, and $\frac{5}{2}$. The distance between the two centers is $\frac{5}{2}$ and the larger radius is $\frac{3}{2}$, so the smaller radius is $\frac{5}{2} - \frac{3}{2} = \boxed{1}$.

Problem 2-5

Method I: Clearly, it is more likely that 2 girls leave than that 2 boys go, so the question is whether it is more likely that 2 girls leave or that 1 boy and 1 girl leave. The probability that 2 girls go is $\left(\frac{10}{15}\right)\left(\frac{9}{14}\right) = \frac{9}{21}$; but the probability that 1 boy and 1 girl leave is $\left(\frac{10}{15}\right)\left(\frac{5}{14}\right) + \left(\frac{5}{15}\right)\left(\frac{10}{14}\right) = \frac{10}{21}$. Since it is more likely that 1 boy and 1 girl leave, it is most likely that 9 girls and 4 boys remain. The answer is 9:4 or $\boxed{\frac{9}{4}}$.

Method II: There are $\frac{10!}{8!2!} = 45$ ways to choose 2 of 10 girls, $\frac{5!}{3!2!} = 10$ ways to choose 2 of 5 boys, and $5 \times 10 = 50$ ways to choose 1 boy and 1 girl. The probability that 1 boy and 1 girl leave is $\frac{50}{45 + 10 + 50} = \frac{10}{21}$.

Problem 2-6

We must solve $(x-6)(x+14) = y^2$ in non-negative integers. Expanding the left side, $x^2 + 8x - 84 = y^2$, and then $x^2 + 8x = y^2 + 84$. Completing the square, $(x+4)^2 = y^2 + 10^2$. Now:

Method I: Since x is a positive integer and y is an integer, either $x = 6$ (and $y = 0$), or we look for Pythagorean triangles with a leg of 10. There is only one: doubling 5-12-13, we will get 10-24-26, and $x = 22$ (with $y = 24$). The possible integral values of x are $\boxed{6,\ 22}$.

Method II: Write $(x+4)^2 = y^2 + 10^2$ as $(x+4)^2 - y^2 = 10^2$. Factor to get $(x+4+y)(x+4-y) = 100$. Now, factor 100 and set $x+4+y$ equal to one factor and $x+4-y$ equal to the other. If $x+4+y = 50$ and $x+4-y = 2$, then $x = 22$ and $y = 24$. If $x+4+y = 10$ and $x+4-y = 10$, then $x = 6$ and $y = 0$. For no other combination of factors of 100 will we get a different positive integral value for x.

Contests written and compiled by Steven R. Conrad & Daniel Flegler   Mathematics Leagues Inc., © 1988

Problem 3-1

Starting with 9^0, the powers of 9 are 1, 9, 81, 729, ..., a sequence whose terms have units' digits which are alternately 1 and 9. Therefore the units' digit of the sum of the first n terms is 1 if n is odd, and 0 if n is even. We are asked to find the units' digit of the sum of the first 1990 terms, so the answer is $\boxed{0}$.

Problem 3-2

Finkin disagrees with Winkin and Blinkin, so each claims a different number of liars. Only one of these claims can be truthful, so the number of liars is $\boxed{2}$.

Problem 3-3

If $x \geq 0$, the equation becomes $x + x = 0$, which is true only when $x = 0$. If $x \leq 0$, the equation becomes $x - x = 0$, which is always true. Therefore the original equation is satisfied as long as $\boxed{x \leq 0}$.

Problem 3-4

Method I: By the definition of inverse functions, $f[f^{-1}(x)] = x$. Since $y = ax+b$, y will be its own inverse if and only if $a(ax+b)+b = x$ for all x. Expanding, $a^2x+ab+b = x$. If this is valid for all x, then $a^2 = 1$. If $a = 1$, then $b = 0$ (and the function is $y = x$). If $a = -1$, then b can be any real number (and the function is $y = -x+b$). This will be perpendicular to $y = x$; so it coincides with its inverse. The answer:

> i) (1,0) and two pairs of the form $(-1,b)$, with b any real number;
> *or*
> ii) three pairs of the form: $(-1,b)$.

Method II: If $y = ax+b$, then, for the inverse, $ay+b = x$—so $y = x/a - b/a$. The function and its inverse

are equal if and only if $a = 1/a$ and $b = -b/a$. Thus, $a^2 = 1$ and $a = \pm 1$. If $a = 1$, then $b = -b$, so $b = 0$. If $a = -1$, then b may be any real number.

Problem 3-5

Multiply on the right side first. The product of the rightmost two factors is easier to get if you notice their radicands are conjugates of each other. Their product is $\sqrt{2 - \sqrt{2+\sqrt{3}}}$. Now we'll multiply this result by the third factor from the right (note that the radicands of these two factors are conjugates). Their product is $\sqrt{2-\sqrt{3}}$. Now, multiply this product by the first factor (again the radicands are conjugates) and their product is 1; so the larger root is 1. Now substitute $x = 1$ into $x^2+4x+k = 0$ to get $k = \boxed{-5}$.

Problem 3-6

Method I: In the diagram at the right, the centers of the circles are B and D and the circles intersect at points A and O. By SSS, $\triangle DOB \cong \triangle DAB$, so both $\angle DOB$ 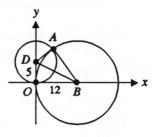 and $\angle DAB$ are right angles. A circle can always be circumscribed about a quadrilateral with supplementary opposite angles, so a circle which passes through points B, A, and O also passes through point D. Since $\overline{DB}$ will be a diameter of this circle, and since $DB = 13$, a radius of this circle will be $\boxed{\frac{13}{2}}$.

Method II: The perpendicular bisector of $\overline{OB}$ is $x = 6$. The perpendicular bisector of $\overline{AO}$ is line DB. Its equation is $y = -5x/12 + 5$. The point $(6, 5/2)$, at which $\overline{AO}$ intersects $\overline{DB}$, is the center of the circumscribed circle. The distance from $(6, 5/2)$ to $(0,0)$ is $13/2$, the radius of the circumscribed circle.

Contests written and compiled by Steven R. Conrad & Daniel Flegler   Mathematics Leagues Inc., © 1989

Problem 4-1

Method I: The symmetrical nature of the equations suggests trying $x = y = z$, and so $(x,y,z) = \boxed{(3,3,3)}$.

Method II: We'll prove that $(3,3,3)$ is the only solution. Add the fractions on the left side of the second equation to get $\frac{xy + xz + yz}{xyz} = 1$, so $xyz = 27$. By the relationship between the roots and coefficients of any cubic equation, x, y, and z are the three roots of the cubic equation $r^3 - 9r^2 + 27r - 27 = 0$. Thus, $(r-3)^3 = 0$, $r = 3$, all three roots are 3, and $(x,y,z) = (3,3,3)$.

Problem 4-2

The sum of the one even number (2) and the twenty odd numbers (the others) is always even, so the correct answer was obtained by $\boxed{\text{Sandy}}$.

Problem 4-3

To get any term from the previous term, multiply the numerator by 19.89 and multiply the denominator by the exponent of the new numerator. The terms formed this way keep getting larger until we multiply by the factor $\frac{19.89}{20}$, and then they begin to decrease. Thus, the term with the largest value is the $\boxed{\text{19th}}$.

Problem 4-4

For the complex number $x+yi$, the absolute value is $\sqrt{x^2+y^2}$. Since $1-2i$ and 5 have different moduli (absolute values), like powers of these two numbers will have different moduli; and, consequently, the powers will not be equal unless the exponent is $\boxed{0}$.

Problem 4-5

Method I: If two figures are similar and the ratio of their linear dimensions is r, then the ratio of the areas of the figures will be r^2, and the ratio of the volumes will be r^3. Since the cubes are similar and the ratio of their areas is $4:1 = 2^2:1$, the ratio of their edges is $2:1$. Thus, their volumes will have the ratio $2^3:1^3 = 8:1$. Since we need to form 4 big cubes, the number of smaller cubes we need is $8 \times 4 = \boxed{32}$.

Method II: Since $64 \div 16 = 4$, 4 small cubes will "fill up" one face of a bigger cube. We need 2 layers of 4 cubes each—8 small cubes for each big cube.

Problem 4-6

In $\frac{7}{10} < \frac{A}{B} < \frac{11}{15}$, both A and B are positive integers, so we can multiply through by $30B$ to get the equivalent inequality $21B < 30A < 22B$. If $B = 1$, A will not be integral. The first value of B for which there is a multiple of 30 between $21B$ and $22B$ is $B = 7$. In that case, $147 < 150 < 154$, so $(A,B) = \boxed{(5,7)}$.

[**NOTE 1:** There are 56 solutions for $\frac{A}{B}$ where B is a positive integer no more than 60. The next 3 "smallest" solutions are $\frac{8}{11}$, $\frac{10}{14}$, and $\frac{12}{17}$.]

[**NOTE 2:** The *mediant* of $\frac{a}{b}$ and $\frac{c}{d}$ is $\frac{a+c}{b+d}$. The mediant of two positive fractions always has a value *between* the two fractions! Using the symbol $\star$ to denote taking the mediant, $\frac{7}{10} \star \frac{11}{15} = \frac{18}{25}$; so $\frac{18}{25}$ lies between $\frac{7}{10}$ and $\frac{11}{15}$. Repeating this, $\frac{7}{10} \star \frac{18}{25} = \frac{25}{35} = \frac{5}{7}$, the "smallest"! It is of interest to note that $\frac{7}{10} \star \frac{5}{7} = \frac{12}{17}$, and $\frac{5}{7} \star \frac{11}{15} = \frac{8}{11}$, and that $\frac{12}{17}$ and $\frac{8}{11}$ are both included on the list of the "smallest" answers.]

Contests written and compiled by Steven R. Conrad & Daniel Flegler   Mathematics Leagues Inc., © 1989

Problem 5-1

Since 20 books cost $260, and 16 books cost $256, it's cheaper to buy 20 books than it is to buy n books if $n = \boxed{17, 18, 19}$.

Problem 5-2

Simplify to get: $1989^{100} = 1989^{x^2}$. Equating exponents, $x^2 = 100$, and $x = \boxed{10, -10}$.

Problem 5-3

Method I: To maximize the number of nickels, we should use nickels and pennies and no other coins. Since $n+p = 48$ and $5n+p = 100$, $n = \boxed{13}$.

Method II: With fewer than 35 pennies, each remaining coin would have an average value of less than 5¢, an impossibility. With 35 pennies, the value of the remaining 13 coins would be 65¢; so their average value would be 5¢ and we'd need 13 nickels.

Problem 5-4

Since $b > 0$, our concern is with the graph as it appears in quadrants I and II. In quadrant I, since $x > 0$, $y = -2x+b$. In quadrant II, since $x < 0$, $y = -2(-x)+b = 2x+b$. Since these lines have y-intercepts of b, and since each has $|\text{slope}| = 2$, they each cross the y-axis b units above the origin and cross the x-axis $\frac{1}{2}b$ units from the origin. The result is an isosceles triangle with an altitude of length b (on the y-axis) and a base of length b (on the x-axis). The area of this triangle is $\frac{1}{2}(b)(b) = \frac{1}{2}b^2 = 72$. Therefore, $b = \boxed{12}$.

Problem 5-5

Since the diagonals of a rectangle are congruent, $PR = QC = 10 = $ the length of a radius of circle C. Since the perimeter of the rectangle is 26, $PC + CR = 13$. Now, since $AC + CB = 20$, $AP + BR = (AC + CB) - (PC + CR) = 20 - 13 = 7$. So far, $AP + PR + BR = 7+10 = 17$. The length of $\overset{\frown}{AQB}$ is 5π (one-quarter the circumference of the circle), so the perimeter is $\boxed{5\pi+17}$.

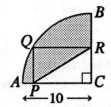

Problem 5-6

If $x = 1$, both sides equal 0; so $x = 1$ is one root of the equation. If $x \neq 1$, then divide both sides of the equation by the product $\log_2 x \log_4 x \log_6 x$. The result is $1 = \frac{1}{\log_6 x} + \frac{1}{\log_4 x} + \frac{1}{\log_2 x}$. For $a,b > 0$ and $a,b \neq 1$, there is a theorem that states that $\frac{1}{\log_b a} = \log_a b$, so $1 = \log_x 6 + \log_x 4 + \log_x 2 = \log_x 48$. Therefore, the two solutions are $x = \boxed{1, 48}$.

[NOTE: If the bases of the logarithms were a, b, and c, then $x = abc$ is one solution—and $x = 1$ is the other solution.]

Contests written and compiled by Steven R. Conrad & Daniel Flegler   Mathematics Leagues Inc., © 1989

Problem 6-1

The value of $b > 0$ for which $x^2 + 2bx + b^2 = x^2 + 2bx + b^3$ also satisfies $b^2 = b^3$. This value is $b = \boxed{1}$.

Problem 6-2

Since $m+1 = 2(h-1)$ and $m-1 = h+1$, $h = \boxed{5}$.

Problem 6-3

Method I: Since A and B are both positive, A will be greater than B if $A^2 > B^2$. Since $A^2 = 19 + 89 + 2\sqrt{19 \times 89} = 108 + 2\sqrt{19 \times 89}$, and $B^2 = 18 + 90 + 2\sqrt{18 \times 90} = 108 + 2\sqrt{18 \times 90}$, we know that $A^2 > B^2$. Therefore, the larger of the two is $\boxed{A}$.

Method II: The graph of $y = \sqrt{x}$ is steep near $x = 0$, and flattens to the right. The difference between "consecutive" square roots decreases as the integers get larger. Hence, $\sqrt{19} - \sqrt{18} > \sqrt{90} - \sqrt{89}$, so $A > B$.

Problem 6-4

Tangents to a circle from the same outside point have equal lengths, so the segments are congruent as shown. Any quadrilateral which can have an inscribed circle also has the sums of the lengths of its opposite

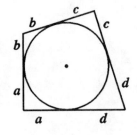

sides equal. [In the diagram shown, the sum of the lengths of each pair of opposite sides is $a+b+c+d$.] In this problem, $4 + 16 = 9 + x$. Solving, $x = \boxed{11}$.

Problem 6-5

Method I: Use the substitution of $\sin\left(\frac{1}{2}\pi - \frac{\pi}{7}\right)$ for $\cos\left(\frac{\pi}{7}\right)$. Then, since $k = \frac{1}{2} - \frac{\pi}{7}$, we get $k = \boxed{\frac{5}{14}}$.

Method II: Since $\operatorname{Arc}\sin\left(\cos\frac{\pi}{7}\right) = k\pi$, taking the sine of each side (using the fact that $\sin[\operatorname{Arc}\sin x] = x$), we get $\cos\frac{\pi}{7} = \sin k$. Because of principal values, $\frac{\pi}{7} + k\pi = \frac{\pi}{2}$ and $k = \frac{5}{14}$.

Problem 6-6

Method I: All the workers mowed the larger field for half a day, and half the workers continued mowing there for another half day, so it follows that $1\frac{1}{2}$ times as many workers as there were could mow the larger field in half a day. Thus, half the workers can mow $\frac{1}{3}$ of the larger field in half a day. The smaller field is half the size of the larger—but the group sent to mow it can mow only $\frac{1}{3}$ of the larger field in the half day they worked on the smaller field. Thus, they left unmowed a section equivalent to $\frac{1}{2} - \frac{1}{3} = \frac{1}{6}$ of the *larger* field. Since this took one worker exactly one day to mow, it follows that one worker can mow $\frac{1}{6}$ of the larger field in 1 day. On the first day, the workers mowed the larger field plus an amount equivalent to $\frac{1}{3}$ of the larger field: a total of $\frac{4}{3} = \frac{8}{6}$ of the larger field. The number of workers was therefore $\boxed{8}$.

Method II: Let the area that 1 worker can mow in 1 day be m. In $\frac{1}{2}$ day, w workers can mow an area of $\frac{1}{2}wm$. In the second half of the day, $\frac{1}{2}$ the team worked on the larger field; so the area of the larger field is $\frac{1}{2}wm + \frac{1}{4}wm = \frac{3wm}{4}$. Also, the area mowed by $\frac{1}{2}w$ workers, who have mowed the smaller field for $\frac{1}{2}$ day, is $\frac{1}{4}wm$. Since 1 worker could mow the uncut portion of the smaller field in 1 day, the uncut portion had an area of m. Thus, the area of the smaller field is $\frac{1}{4}wm + m$. The area of the first field is twice that of the second, so $\frac{3wm}{4} = 2(\frac{1}{4}wm + m)$, and $w = 8$.

Problem 1-1

Since the two squares are congruent, the length of each side must be 6. The rectangle's dimensions are 6 by 12, and its perimeter must be $\boxed{36}$.

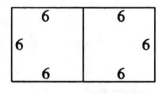

Problem 1-2

The information in the problem is equivalent to the algebraic equation $\frac{1}{x} = \frac{1}{2}+\frac{1}{3}+\frac{1}{6} = 1$. Thus, $x = \boxed{1}$.

Problem 1-3

When N is even and divisible by 4, then N^2 will be divisible by 16 (and, hence, by 8). When N is even but *not* divisible by 4, then N^2 will be divisible by 4, but *not* by 8. Of the 994 even integers from 1 to 1989, half are divisible by 4. The probability is $\boxed{\frac{1}{2}}$.

Problem 1-4

Let the distances from the worm to the trees be called x and y. The birds flew equal distances, so the triangles have congruent hypotenuses, and $x^2+10^2 =$

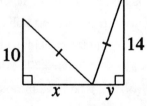

y^2+14^2, or $x^2-y^2 = 96 = (x+y)(x-y)$. Since $x+y = 16$, it follows that $x-y = 6$ and, then, $x = \boxed{11}$.

Problem 1-5

Rewriting, $3^{2\sqrt{3x}}+3 = 4(3^{\sqrt{3x}})$. If we let $y = 3^{\sqrt{3x}}$, then $y^2-4y+3 = 0$. Solving, $y = 3$ or 1, so $\sqrt{3x} = 1$ or 0. The respective values of x are $\boxed{\frac{1}{3}, \, 0}$.

Problem 1-6

We'll solve this by using a chain of equations. We start with $2000! = k(1000!)[1\times3\times5\times\ldots\times1999] = k(1\times2\times\ldots\times1000)[1\times3\times\ldots\times1999] = k(\frac{1}{2}\times2)\times(\frac{1}{2}\times4)\times\ldots\times(\frac{1}{2}\times2000)[1\times3\times\ldots\times1999] = \frac{k}{2^{1000}}(2\times4\times6\times\ldots\times2000)[1\times3\times\ldots\times1999] = \frac{k}{2^{1000}}[1\times2\times\ldots\times1999\times2000] = \frac{k}{2^{1000}}[2000!]$. Hence, $k = \boxed{2^{1000}}$.

Contests written and compiled by Steven R. Conrad & Daniel Flegler   **Mathematics Leagues Inc., © 1989**

Problem 2-1

Since $A = 9^{1989}$ and $B = (-9)^{1989}$, $A+B = 0$, and $(1+9+8+9)^0 = \boxed{1}$.

Problem 2-2

Method I: Divide $10.00 by 23¢, and the remainder is 11¢, which isn't divisible by 17¢. With one fewer 23¢ item, the remainder would have been 11¢ + 23¢ = 34¢. Dividing 34¢ by 17¢, the quotient is $\boxed{2}$.

Method II: Let s and t be the respective number of 17¢ and 23¢ items sold. Then $17s+23t = 1000$. Since $17+23 = 40$ and $1000 \div 40 = 25$, $(25,25)$ is a solution of $17s+23t = 1000$. The graph of $t = -\frac{17s}{23} + \frac{1000}{23}$ goes through the lattice point $(25,25)$. Since its slope is $-\frac{17}{23}$, the line goes through every point with coordinates $(25-23k, 25+17k)$. For the required value of s, let $k = 1$.

Problem 2-3

The shortest distance between the endpoints of any line segment of length x is x, so $3+4+5 > x$. The greatest integral value of x is $\boxed{11}$.

Problem 2-4

Method I: There are n female dancers. In sequence:
    1st, Mary danced with $6+1$ partners;
    2nd, Lisa danced with $6+2$ partners;
    . . . .
    nth, Jill danced with $6+n$ partners.
So $n+6+n = 20$, $n = 7$, and the number of male partners was $20-7 = \boxed{13}$.

Method II: Solving $m-f = 6$ and $m+f = 20$, $m = 13$.

Problem 2-5

Method I: Letting $y = x+1$, we get $(y+1)^4+(y-1)^4 = 82$, or $y^4+6y^2-40 = (y^2+10)(y^2-4) = 0$. The real

solutions, obtained from $y^2 = 4$, are $x = \boxed{1, -3}$.

Method II: $(x+2)^4+x^4 = (\pm 3)^4+(\pm 1)^4$. If $x+2 = 3$, then $x = 1$; if $x+2 = -1$, then $x = -3$, and both values check. The other possibilities fail to check. The graphs of $y = (x+2)^4$ and $y = 82-x^4$ intersect twice, so there are only two real roots.

Method III: Expanding, $2x^4+8x^3+24x^2+32x-66 = 0$. By the Rational Root Theorem, $2(x-1)(x+3)(x^2+2x+11) = 0$. The real roots are $x = 1$, $x = -3$.

Problem 2-6

Method I: Each segment connecting a vertex of the inner triangle to the corresponding vertex of the outer triangle passes through a vertex of the middle triangle. [For a proof, note that each middle 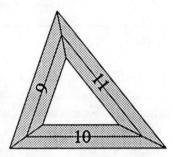 vertex is equidistant from two sides of the outer triangle; and each innermost vertex is equidistant from two sides of the middle triangle. Thus, all three corresponding vertices lie on the same angle bisector of the outer triangle.] Draw these segments to get three trapezoids together with their medians. The altitude (h) of each trapezoid is 2. The lengths of the medians (m) are 9, 10, and 11. The area we want is the sum of the areas of the three trapezoids. The area of each trapezoid is hm, so the sum is $2(9+10+11) = \boxed{60}$.

[**NOTE:** In *any* such figure, even with circles, the area = (width of the "ring")(perimeter of the mid-figure).]

Method II: Rearrange the three "pieces" as shown.

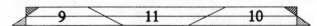

The equidistant parallel lines guarantee the congruences needed to make the trapezoids and the 30×2 rectangle have the same areas of 60.

Contests written and compiled by Steven R. Conrad & Daniel Flegler   Mathematics Leagues Inc., © 1989

Problem 3-1

Let A, B, K represent the respective number of cents that Ali, Brian and Keith have. But $A = K+20$ and $B = K+60$, so $A+B+K = 3K+80 = 100D$. For K and D to be whole numbers, D is at least $\boxed{2}$.

Problem 3-2

The diagonals of an inscribed rectangle cross at the center of its circumscribed circle, so this circle's radius is 10 and its area is $\boxed{100\pi}$.

Problem 3-3

Method I: If Hocus lied, he'd be the oldest, but all 3 would be liars—so Hocus told the truth and the others lied. From Crocus' lie and Hocus' statement, Hocus is not the youngest or oldest. From Pocus' lie, Crocus isn't oldest, so the youngest is $\boxed{\text{Crocus}}$.

Method II: From youngest to oldest, the possibilities are: 1)CHP, 2)CPH, 3)HCP, 4)HPC, 5)PCH, 6)PHC. Pocus is truthful in only 4 and 6, Crocus in only 3 and 4, and Hocus in only 1, 3, 4, and 6. The only possibility consistent with all requirements is 1)CHP.

Problem 3-4

The solution $(100,1)$ is obvious if 1990 is read as "nineteen hundred ninety." To find other solution:

Method I: If $1990 = (19\times100)+(90\times1)$, then $1990 = (19\times100)-(19\times90)+(19\times90)+(90\times1) = 19(100-90)+90(19+1) = (19\times10)+(90\times20)$. The 2 solutions are $\boxed{(100,1), (10,20)}$.

Method II: As in Method II for problem 2-2 of last month: Since $(100,1)$ is a solution of $19x+90y = 1990$, the graph of $y = -\frac{19x}{90} + \frac{1990}{90}$ goes through the point $(100,1)$. The slope of this line is $-\frac{19}{90}$, so it passes through any point whose coordinates are $(100-90k, 1+19k)$. For the other solution use the value $k = 1$.

Problem 3-5

Since $x+y = 5^{x-y}$ is equivalent to the first equation, we may replace $x+y$ in the second equation to get $5^{(x-y)^2} = 5$. From this, $(x-y)^2 = 1$. Now, if $x-y = 1$, then $x+y = 5$. But, if $x-y = -1$, then $x+y = \frac{1}{5}$. Therefore, $(x,y) = \boxed{(3,2),(-\frac{2}{5},\frac{3}{5})}$.

Problem 3-6

Method I: Since $f(x) = x^2-x+1$ has a negative discriminant, its graph will not cross the x-axis. Since $f(0)$ is 1, f is positive, so we may multiply through by f to get the equivalent inequality $-3x^2+3x-3 < x^2+px-2 < 2x^2-2x+2$. The left-hand inequality is equivalent to $4x^2+(p-3)x+1 > 0$. The right-hand inequality is equivalent to $x^2-(p+2)x+4 > 0$. These two inequalities hold for *all* real x if and only if the discriminants of both quadratics are negative; that is, if $(p-3)^2-16 < 0$ and $(p+2)^2-16 < 0$. Equivalently, $|p-3| < 4$ and $|p+2| < 4$. Combine the inequalities $-1 < p < 7$ and $-6 < p < 2$ to get the result $\boxed{-1 < p < 2}$.

Method II: This solution is Method I, but we won't use the discriminant. Since $x^2-x+1 = (x-\frac{1}{2})^2+\frac{3}{4}$, $f(x) > 0$. Next, $y = 4x^2+(p-3)x+1$ is a parabola with its vertex a minimum at $x = \frac{3-p}{8}$. Thus, $4x^2+(p-3)x+1 > 0$ or $(p-3)^2-16 < 0$. The minimum point of $y = x^2-(p+2)x+4$ is at $x = \frac{p+2}{2}$; and if $x^2-(p+2)x+4 > 0$, then $(p+2)^2-16 < 0$.

Contests written and compiled by Steven R. Conrad & Daniel Flegler   Mathematics Leagues Inc., ©1990

Problem 4-1

Factoring, the left–hand side becomes $\frac{x}{5}(1+\frac{1}{2}+\frac{1}{3}+\frac{1}{4})$. Therefore, the two sides will be equal if $x = \boxed{5}$.

Problem 4-2

Method I: To do this algebraically, let ab, bc, cd, ad denote the respective signed distances of AB, BC, CD, AD. Then $ab = \pm3$, $bc = \pm4$, $cd = \pm5$. But, $AD = |ad| = |ab+bc+cd| = |\pm3\pm4\pm5|$, so AD's minimum value is $|3+4-5| = \boxed{2}$.

Method II: The diagram below shows how to minimize AD, and we see that $AD = 2$.

Problem 4-3

Method I: Since there are equal numbers of cards of both colors, there are as many red cards in the top half as there are black cards in the bottom half. Hence, the number of red cards in the top half is $30\div2 = \boxed{15}$.

Method II: If there are r red cards in the top half, then there are $26-r$ red cards in the bottom half. Hence there are $26-(26-r) = r$ black cards in the bottom half, so $r+r = 30$, and $r = 15$.

Problem 4-4

Method I: The given inequality says that $|x|$ is less than 14 units from 5. Since $|x|$ is non-negative, it follows that $0 \le |x| < 19$, so $\boxed{-19 < x < 19}$.

Method II: The given inequality becomes $-14 < 5-|x| < 14$, or $-19 < -|x| < 9$ or finally, $-9 <|x| < 19$. Since $-9 < |x|$ is always true, the only condition that remains is $|x| < 19$, so $-19 < x < 19$.

Problem 4-5

If we substitute $\sin^2x+\cos^2x = 1$, $\tan^2x = \sec^2x-1$, and $\cot^2x = \csc^2x-1$ into the original equation and then simplify the result, we get $\sec^2x+\csc^2x = 16$. Now, convert to $\sin x$ and $\cos x$, add the fractions that result, replace $\sin^2x+\cos^2x$ with 1, and take reciprocals to get $\sin^2x\cos^2x = \frac{1}{16}$, or $4\sin^2x\cos^2x = \frac{1}{4}$. Since $\sin 2x = 2\sin x\cos x$, this can be rewritten as $\sin^22x = \frac{1}{4}$. Since x must be acute, $\sin 2x = \frac{1}{2}$, so $2x = 30°$ or $150°$. Solving, we find $x = \boxed{15°, 75°}$.

Problem 4-6

Method I: Since every parallelogram is symmetric about the intersection of its diagonals, any line which divides the parallelogram into two regions of equal area must pass through this intersection point. This point is $(3,1)$, the midpoint of the diagonals. Since t passes through the points $(3,1)$ and $(1989,1990)$, the slope of t is $\frac{1989}{1986}$, or $\boxed{\frac{663}{662}}$.

Method II: The parallelogram has vertices $A(0,0)$, $B(4,0)$, $C(6,2)$, and $D(2,2)$. There must exist a point $E(x,0)$ at which line t crosses the x-axis. For the parallelogram to be split equally, the distance from $A(0,0)$ to $E(x,0)$ must equal the distance from $C(6,2)$ to $F(6-x,2)$. Since E, F, and $P(1989,1990)$ are collinear, we can solve for x.

Contests written and compiled by Steven R. Conrad & Daniel Flegler　　Mathematics Leagues Inc., © 1990

Contest # 5 — *Answers & Solutions* — 3/6/90

Problem 5-1

Since $x^2+5x+6 = (x+2)(x+3)$, the two ordered pairs are $\boxed{(-2,-3),(-3,-2)}$.

Problem 5-2

Rejecting the numbers $1990+d$ that are obviously composite, the values of d that remain are 1, 3, 7, and 9. Since 11 divides 1991, the primes are 1993, 1997, 1999; so the sum is $3+7+9 = \boxed{19}$.

Problem 5-3

Method I: As seen in the diagram, the areas of the small rectangles are ac, bc, ad, and bd. The product of the areas of rectangles *I* and *IV* equals the product of the areas of *II* and *III*. Solving $6x = (2)(3)$, $3x = (2)(6)$, and $2x = (3)(6)$, we see that $x = \boxed{1, 4, 9}$.

Method II: We may label the rectangles as shown in the diagrams below and calculate the possible area of the fourth rectangle from the lengths indicated.

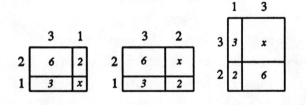

Problem 5-4

Method I: Let $2x-1800 = y$. Then $2y-1800 = z$ and $2z-1800 = 0$. Solving, $z = 900$, $y = 1350$, and $x = \boxed{1575}$.

Method II: If I begin with x, then double my money, then lose $1800, then after 3 rounds I can find x from $2[2(2x-1800)-1800]-1800 = r$, where r is what remains. If $r = 0$, $x = 1575$.

Method III: Work backwards from the *end*:

MONEY LEFT AFTER THE EVENT

EVENT	Round 1	Round 2	Round 3
Start	$1575	$1350	$900
Doubled	3150	2700	1800
Lost $1800	1350	900	0 *end*

Method IV: Work forwards, as usual:

MONEY LEFT AFTER THE EVENT

EVENT	Round 1	Round 2	Round 3
Start	x	$2x-y$	$4x-3y$
Doubled	$2x$	$4x-2y$	$8x-6y$
Lost y	$2x-y$	$4x-3y$	$8x-7y$ *end*

Now, solve $8x-7y = 0$ [with $y = 1800$].

Problem 5-5

Method I: There are equal numbers of subsets with n and $5-n$ elements for $n = 0,1,2,3,4,5$. Thus, the average number of elements in each of the subsets is $2\frac{1}{2}$. The total is $32(2\frac{1}{2}) = \boxed{80}$.

Method II: $\binom{5}{0}, \binom{5}{1}, \binom{5}{2}, \binom{5}{3}, \binom{5}{4}, \binom{5}{5}$ represent the respective number of 0, 1, 2, 3, 4, 5-element subsets, and $1\times0+5\times1+10\times2+10\times3+5\times4+1\times5 = 80$.

Problem 5-6

Method I: Use the change of base theorem: $\log ab = \frac{\log b}{\log a}$. Then, multiply the equations respectively by $2\log 3$, $2\log 4$, and $2\log 5$ to get $\log x+\log y+2\log z = 4\log 3$, $\log x+2\log y+\log z = 4\log 2$, and $2\log x+\log y +\log z = 0$. Add these, then divide by 4: $\log x+\log y+\log z = \log 2+\log 3$. Subtract this from the 3rd equation above: $\log x = -\log 2 -\log 3$, so $x = \boxed{\frac{1}{6}}$.

Method II: $\log_{25}x^2 = \log_5 x$, $\log_{16}y^2 = \log_4 y$ and $\log_9 z^2 = \log_3 z$; so $xyz^2 = 81$, $xy^2z = 16$, and $x^2yz = 1$. Multiplying, $x^4y^4z^4 = 2^4 3^4$; so $xyz = 6$, $x = \frac{x^2yz}{xyz} = \frac{1}{6}$. Similarly, $y = \frac{8}{3}$ and $z = \frac{27}{2}$.

Contests written and compiled by Steven R. Conrad & Daniel Flegler   Mathematics Leagues Inc., © 1990

Problem 6-1

Since $22^2 \times 55^2 = 2^2 \times 11^2 \times 5^2 \times 11^2 = 2^2 \times 5^2 \times 11^2 \times 11^2 = 10^2 \times 121^2 = 10^2 \times N^2$, and $N > 0$, $N = \boxed{121}$.

Problem 6-2

Each of the arcs is a 90° arc, so each chord is one side of a square inscribed in a circle whose diameter is 16. The length of each chord is $\boxed{8\sqrt{2}}$.

Problem 6-3

The sum of the probabilities is 1, so $6p^2 + p = 1$, and $(3p-1)(2p+1) = 0$. Since $p \geq 0$, we obtain $p = \boxed{\frac{1}{3}}$.

Problem 6-4

Since $1+2+\ldots+n = \frac{1}{2}n(n+1)$, the original equation can be written as $\frac{1}{2}n(n+1) = 100n$ or $n^2 - 199n = 0$. Since $n > 0$, $n = 199$ and $10n = \boxed{1990}$.

Problem 6-5

Method I: If t is the number of hours I need to arrive on time, then $20(t+1) = 30(t-1)$, so $t = 5$. Since $20(t+1) = kt$, we get $k = \boxed{24}$.

Method II: Since $t = d/20 - 1 = d/30 + 1$, $d = 120$ km and $t = 5$ hrs. Finally, $k = d/t = 24$ km/hr.

Method III: Suppose, for *both* the early and late arrivals, I'd traveled exactly the amount of time I needed when traveling at k km/hr—not 1 hour less and 1 hour more. Then, the points where I'd have stopped would have been 30 km + 20 km = 50 km apart. But 30 km/hr − 20 km/hr = 10 km/hr, so the distances traveled at these rates differ by 10 km each hour traveled. Since distance ÷ rate = time, $\frac{50 \ km}{10 \ km/hr}$

= 5 hours is the time normally needed. [Numerically, the time normally needed, in hours, is the sum of the rates ÷ by their difference.] Continue as in Method I.

Method IV: Let d be the required distance (in km). The *time* traveled at k km/hr is the average of the *times* traveled at 20 km/hr and 30 km/hr. Hence, $\frac{d}{k} = \frac{\frac{d}{20} + \frac{d}{30}}{2}$, $\frac{2}{k} = \frac{1}{20} + \frac{1}{30}$, $k = \frac{2 \times 20 \times 30}{20+30}$. This value of k is known as the *harmonic mean* of 20 and 30. It is independent of t and d!

Method V: Going there at 20 km/hr and returning at 30 km/hr takes the same total time as a roundtrip at k km/hr. This situation is a special case of the problem: "If I drive out at x km/hr and back at y km/hr, what's my average rate for the round trip?" The answer is the *harmonic mean* of x and y, $\frac{2xy}{x+y}$.

Problem 6-6

Method I: Since $1+\omega+\omega^2 = 0$, we get $1+\omega-\omega^2 = -2\omega^2$ and also $1-\omega+\omega^2 = -2\omega$. The value sought is then $(-2\omega)^3 + (-2\omega^2)^3 = -8 \times 1 + -8 \times 1 = \boxed{-16}$.

Method II: If $\omega^3 = 1$, then $(\omega-1)(\omega^2+\omega+1) = 0$. Solving, $\omega = 1$, $\frac{1}{2}(-1+\sqrt{-3})$ or $\frac{1}{2}(-1-\sqrt{-3})$. Each of these last two values is the square of the other, and these values can be used to compute the value sought in the problem.

Method III: Since $\omega^3 = 1$, $\omega^3 - 1 = (\omega-1)(\omega^2+\omega+1) = 0$. Since $\omega \neq 1$, $\omega^2+\omega+1 = 0$. Thus, $1+\omega = -\omega^2$, and $1+\omega^2 = -\omega$. Therefore, $(1+\omega-\omega^2)^3 + (1-\omega+\omega^2)^3 = (-\omega^2-\omega^2)^3 + (-\omega-\omega)^3 = (-2\omega^2)^3 + (-2\omega)^3$. Now, $\omega^3 = 1 = \omega^6$, so $(-2\omega^2)^3 + (-2\omega)^3 = (-8\omega^6) + (-8\omega^3)$, and this sum is −16.

Contests written and compiled by Steven R. Conrad & Daniel Flegler   Mathematics Leagues Inc., © 1990

Problem 1-1

The expression $(B)(\frac{1}{A})$ is the reciprocal of the expression $(A)(\frac{1}{B})$. Hence, since $(A)(\frac{1}{B}) = 1 + \frac{1}{1990} = \frac{1991}{1990}$, the value of $(B)(\frac{1}{A})$ is $\boxed{\frac{1990}{1991}}$.

Problem 1-2

Let the average of the 20 positive numbers be A and let the sum be S. Since $S = 20A$, the desired percent is $(\frac{20A}{A})(100) = \boxed{2000 \text{ or } 2000\%}$.

Problem 1-3

A side of the smallest square is 4, so A's coordinates are $A(4,0)$. Since a side of the largest square is 12, the coordinates of point B are $B(21-12,12) = B(9,12)$. The distance formula can now be used to calculate the distance from A

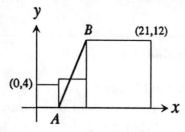

to B. Here's another way to calculate this distance: since a side of the middle square is $21 - 12 - 4 = 5$, the right triangle with hypotenuse AB is a $5-12-13$ triangle, and $AB = \boxed{13}$.

Problem 1-4

If the winner ate x pies, then the runner-up ate $x/2$ pies, the 3rd-place contestant ate $x/3$ pies, and the 4th-place contestant ate $x/4$ pies. The total number of pies eaten was $25x/12$. To make both x and $25x/12$ integral, x must be a multiple of 12. Since $25x/12 < 60$, $x = 12$ or 24, so the maximum value of x is $\boxed{24}$.

[**NOTE:** It is easier to start with $12x$ rather than x.]

Problem 1-5

$$\frac{x}{y} + x = \frac{y}{x} + y \Leftrightarrow x^2 + x^2y = y^2 + xy^2$$
$$\Leftrightarrow x^2 - y^2 = -x^2y + xy^2$$
$$\Leftrightarrow (x+y)(x-y) = -xy(x-y).$$

Since $x \neq y$, $(x-y) \neq 0$, so $x + y = -xy$. Therefore,
$$\frac{1}{x} + \frac{1}{y} = \frac{x+y}{xy} = \frac{-xy}{xy} = \boxed{-1}.$$

Problem 1-6

When we divide one integer by another, the remainder is non-negative and less than the absolute value of the divisor. When dividing an age greater than 6 into five consecutive integers, the remainders will be five consecutive integers, *unless* one of the five dividends is a multiple of the age. Each age is greater than 6, since division by 6 (or a smaller number) gives remainders whose sum is at most $1+2+3+4+5 = 15 < 32$. If none of the consecutive integers is a multiple of an age, we can represent the remainders as y, $y+1$, $y+2$, $y+3$, and $y+4$. Their sum is $5y+10$. But y is an integer, so this cannot equal 32. Therefore, one remainder is 0, and one of the consecutive integers is a multiple of an age. If the first integer were a multiple of an age, the remainders would be 0, 1, 2, 3, and 4. Their sum is 10. Since the sum of the remainders is 32, the first integer is not a multiple of an age. Let an age be x. If the second integer were a multiple of x, then the remainders would be $x-1$, 0, 1, 2, and 3. Their sum is $x+5 = 32$; so $x = 27$. (The integers are 26, 27, 28, 29, and 30. More generally, they are $27k-1$, $27k$, $27k+1$, $27k+2$, and $27k+3$.) If the third integer were a multiple of x, the remainders would be $x-2$, $x-1$, 0, 1, and 2. Their sum is $2x = 32$, so $x = 16$. If the fourth or fifth integer were a multiple of x, the respective remainders would be $x-3$, $x-2$, $x-1$, 0, and 1 (but their sum is $3x-5$, and, since x is integral, this cannot equal 32) or $x-4$, $x-3$, $x-2$, $x-1$, and 0 (but their sum is $4x-10$, and this cannot equal 32). Thus, Al is 16, Sue is 27, and the sum of their ages is $\boxed{43}$.

Contests written and compiled by Steven R. Conrad & Daniel Flegler   Mathematics Leagues Inc., © 1990

Contest # 2   *Answers & Solutions*   **12/4/90**

Problem 2-1

The value of the first expression is $(45)^{1990}$, and the value of the second expression is $(-45)^{1990}$. Since these are equal, their difference is $\boxed{0}$.

Problem 2-2

The sum of the digits of a two-digit number cannot exceed $9+9 = 18$. Since the sum of the digits of the page I was reading was 19, the page number must have had at least 3 digits. The digit-sum of the next page is 2. Since *Alice in Wonderland* has fewer than 1000 pages, its page number is 200; and the page I was reading was page $\boxed{199}$.

[**NOTE #1:** Since we do not require familiarity with the number of pages in *Alice in Wonderland*, we will **also give credit for any answer of the form 1...99,** where the missing digits, if any, are *all* 0's.]

[**NOTE #2:** The page with a digit-sum of 2 *cannot* be of the form $10...010...00 = 10^a + 10^b$, $a > b \geq 3$, since the digit–sum of the previous page would not be 19.]

Problem 2-3

If $\sqrt{x} = x$, then $x = 0$ or 1. Hence, since $\sqrt{a+b} = a+b$, then $a+b = 0$ or 1. Since a and b are non-negative integers, the solutions are $\boxed{(0,0),(1,0),(0,1)}$.

Problem 2-4

Method I: The distance d, satisfies $\frac{d}{3} + \frac{d}{4} = \frac{7}{2}$. Solving, $d = \boxed{6 \text{ or } 6 \text{ km}}$.

Method II: I spent less time at the faster speed and more at the slower speed. The rates were in the ratio 4:3, so the times were in the ratio 3:4. Of the $3\frac{1}{2}$ hrs,

I spent $\frac{3}{7} \times \frac{7}{2} = 1\frac{1}{2}$ hrs at 4 km/h. If I walk at 4 km/h for $1\frac{1}{2}$ hrs, the number of km I walk is $\boxed{6 \text{ or } 6 \text{ km}}$.

Problem 2-5

If the distance to the longer side is x, then the distance to the shorter side is $x+8$. Thus, the shorter dimension of the rectangle will be $2x$, and its longer dimension will be $2(x+8)$. Since the perimeter of the rectangle is 88 cm, 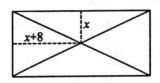 $2(2x+2(x+8)) = 88$. Solving, we get $x = 7$. Hence, the dimensions of the rectangle are 14 and 30, and the area is $14 \times 30 = \boxed{420}$.

Problem 2-6

We will show that, for a quadratic equation with integral coefficients, the discriminant is either a multiple of 4, or 1 more than a multiple of 4. If b is even, then b^2 is a multiple of 4, and $b^2 - 4ac$ is the difference of two multiples of 4; so it too is a multiple of 4. If b is odd, then $b = 2k+1$, so $b^2 = 4(k^2+k)+1 = 4t+1$; thus if b is odd, then b^2 is 1 more than a multiple of 4. Hence, if b is odd, then $D = b^2 - 4ac = 4t + 1 - 4ac = 4(t-ac)+1$ is also 1 more than a multiple of 4. If the discriminant is 49, the roots are rational, not irrational (as required). Neither 50 nor 51 is a multiple of 4, or 1 more than a multiple of 4, so neither 50 nor 51 can be the value of the discriminant of a quadratic equation with integral coefficients. Finally, $x^2 + 8x + 3 = 0$ has a discriminant of 52, so the least value of $D > 48$ for which the solutions of a quadratic equation with integral coefficients will be irrational is $\boxed{52}$.

Contests written and compiled by Steven R. Conrad & Daniel Flegler   **Mathematics Leagues Inc., © 1990**

Problem 3-1

Method I: There are 8 such numbers from 12 to 19, 9 from 21–29 and 31–39, . . . , and 91–99. The total is $8 + (9+9+9+9+9+9+9+9) = 8+72 = \boxed{80}$.

Method II: Excluding 0, $9 \times 9 = 81$ numbers are possible. Disallowing the 11, leaves 80 numbers.

Problem 3-2

Method I: Since $m\angle EAB = m\angle EBA = m\angle EBC = m\angle ECB = m\angle ECD = m\angle EDC = 45°$, and $\overline{AB} \cong \overline{BC} \cong \overline{DC}$, it follows that that $\triangle ABE \cong \triangle BCE \cong \triangle CDE$. Now, since $AC = 12$, $AE = EC = 6 = EB$, and the area of $\triangle BCE$ is $\frac{1}{2}(6)(6) = \boxed{18}$.

Method II: Draw $\overline{AD}$, creating square $ABCD$ whose diagonal is 12. The area of any square is half the product of its diagonals, so the area of $ABCD$ is 72. But $\triangle BCE$ is only $\frac{1}{4}$ of the square, so its area is 18.

Problem 3-3

Since $2^{1990} \times 5^{1991} = 2^{1990} \times 5^{1990} \times 5^1 = 10^{1990} \times 5 = 50...0$, the sum of *all* the digits in the product is $\boxed{5}$.

Problem 3-4

When x is divided by y, the quotient is 3 and the remainder is 7, so $x = 3y+7$. Divide this by $2y$ to get
$$\frac{x}{2y} = \frac{3y}{2y} + \frac{7}{2y} = \frac{2y}{2y} + \frac{y}{2y} + \frac{7}{2y} = 1 + \frac{y+7}{2y}.$$
When we divide x by y, the remainder is 7, so $y > 7$. Since y is integral, $y \geq 8$, making $0 < \frac{y+7}{2y} < 1$. Hence, the quotient, q, is 1 and the remainder, r, is $y+7$. Since $y \geq 8$, the least possible value of r is $\boxed{15}$.

Problem 3-5

Method I: In this progression, with first term a and common difference d, the sum of the third and fifth terms is $a+2d + a+4d = 14$. Simplifying, $a+3d=7$. Next, $129 = a+(a+d)+ \ldots + (a+11d) = 12a+66d = 12a+22(3d) = 12a+22(7-a) = -10a+154$, so $a = 2\frac{1}{2}$ and $d = 1\frac{1}{2}$. Finally, if $193 = a+(n-1)d$, then it follows that $n = \boxed{128}$.

Method II: Since $a+3d$ is the fourth term, and since the value of this term is 7 (see Method I), the first 12 terms are $7-3d, 7-2d, 7-d, 7, 7+d, \ldots, 7+8d$. Their sum is $84+30d = 129$, so $d = 1\frac{1}{2}$. The solution now follows the last sentence of Method I.

Problem 3-6

Method I: Ali wins whenever one of the sequences H, $TTTH$, $TTTTTTH$, . . . occurs: sequences where the first H is preceded by $3n$ T's, whose probability is
$$\left(\frac{1}{2}\right) + \left(\frac{1}{8}\right)\left(\frac{1}{2}\right) + \left(\frac{1}{8}\right)^2\left(\frac{1}{2}\right) + \ldots.$$
This is an infinite geometric series whose sum is $\boxed{\frac{4}{7}}$.

Method II: Let Ali have probability p of winning. If Ali flips a tail on the first round, Bobby *then* finds himself having probability p of winning, for it's as though he's the first player in the game. Since the probability that Ali will flip a tail on round 1 is $\frac{1}{2}$, Bobby's actual probability of winning is $\frac{1}{2}p$. By the same reasoning, Carmen's probability of winning is half that of Bobby's, so Carmen's probability of winning is $\frac{1}{4}p$. Since $p + \frac{1}{2}p + \frac{1}{4}p = 1$, $p = \frac{4}{7}$.

Method III: The possible round 1 flips are $\{HHH, HHT, HTH, HTT, THH, THT, TTH, TTT\}$. Ali wins in the first 4 cases and loses in the next 3. If all three people get tails, the procedure is repeated, *with the same set of possible outcomes*. Since there are only 7 ways in which the game can *end* (the 7 ways listed), Ali's probability of winning is $\frac{4}{7}$.

Contests written and compiled by Steven R. Conrad & Daniel Flegler   Mathematics Leagues Inc., © 1991

Problem 4-1

If I have n books all together, then $n-2$ of them are algebra books, $n-2$ of them are trigonometry books, and $n-2$ of them are geometry books. Since I have n books all together, $n = 3(n-2)$ and $n = \boxed{3}$.

Problem 4-2

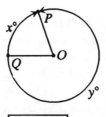

If the degree-measure of the arc traveled by the faster particle is y and the degree-measure of the arc traveled by the slower particle is x, then, $y = 4x$. Since $y + x = 4x + x = 360°$, $m\angle POQ = x = \boxed{72 \text{ or } 72°}$.

Problem 4-3

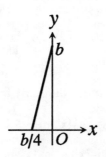

A line with slope 4 which intersects the y-axis at $(0,b)$ will intersect the x-axis at $\left(-\frac{b}{4},0\right)$. Since the area of the triangle is 4, $\frac{1}{2}\left(\frac{1}{4}b\right)(b) = 4$ and $b = \boxed{4\sqrt{2}}$.

Problem 4-4

Rewriting, we see that $1991^{1990} = (1990+1)^{1990} = 1990^{1990}\left(1+\frac{1}{1990}\right)^{1990}$. Since $\lim_{n\to\infty}\left(1+\frac{1}{n}\right)^n = e$, and since the value of this binomial expansion is less than e when $n = 1990$, we get $\left(1+\frac{1}{1990}\right)^{1990} < e < 1990$, so $1990^{1990}\left(1+\frac{1}{1990}\right)^{1990} < 1990^{1990}(1990)$. Since the number on the right is equal to 1990^{1991}, the larger of the two expressions is $\boxed{1990^{1991}}$.

[**NOTE:** We hoped students would use a pattern approach: $2^3 < 3^2$, $3^4 > 4^3$, $4^5 > 5^4$, and, for integral $n > 2$, $n^{(n+1)} > (n+1)^n$, with the gap widening.]

Problem 4-5

Let $f(x) = ax+b$. Since $f(f(x)) = a(ax+b)+b = a^2x+ab+b = 2x+4$, we know $a^2 = 2$. We also know that $ab+b = b(a+1) = 4$, so $b = 4/(a+1)$. If $a = -\sqrt{2}$, then a and b will both be negative, and $f(1) = a+b < 0$. For $f(1)$ to be positive, we must use $a = \sqrt{2}$. Solving for b and rationalizing the denominator, we get $b = 4(\sqrt{2}-1)$. Thus, $f(1) = a+b = \boxed{5\sqrt{2}-4}$.

Problem 4-6

Method I: Multiplying, the product is

$$1 + \frac{1}{2} + \frac{1}{4} + \frac{1}{8} + \frac{1}{16} + \ldots + \left(\frac{1}{2}\right)^{255}.$$

This is a finite geometric progression whose sum is $2-2^{-255}$, so $k = \boxed{-255}$.

Method II: Let $P = (1+x)(1+x^2)\times\ldots\times(1+x^{128})$. Multiplying both sides by $(1-x)$, we get

$$(1-x)P = (1-x)(1+x)(1+x^2)\times\ldots\times(1+x^{128})$$
$$= (1-x^2)(1+x^2)(1+x^4)\times\ldots\times(1+x^{128})$$
$$= (1-x^4)(1+x^4)(1+x^8)\times\ldots\times(1+x^{128})$$
$$\vdots$$
$$= 1 - x^{256}.$$

When $x = \frac{1}{2}$, then $\frac{1}{2}P = 1-\left(\frac{1}{2}\right)^{256}$. If we now multiply by 2, then $P = 2-2^{-255}$; so $k = -255$.

[**NOTE:** Like problem 4-4, pattern searching puts this problem within reach. The first factor is $3/2 = 2-2^{-1}$; the first 2 factors have a product of $15/8 = 2-2^{-3}$; the first 3 factors have a product of $255/128 = 2-2^{-7}$. In absolute value, these exponents are each 1 less than a power of 2; so, for 8 factors, $k = -(2^8-1)$.]

Contests written and compiled by Steven R. Conrad & Daniel Flegler   **Mathematics Leagues Inc., © 1991**

Problem 5-1

If the first year of a decade were the last year of a president's term, then, during the next 8 years, two more presidents would serve. The last year of this decade is the first year of another president's term; so the maximum number of presidents that can hold office during a ten-year period in Oz is $\boxed{4}$.

Problem 5-2

If x is an integer, then $\frac{17}{x}$ will also be an integer if and only if x is a divisor (positive or negative) of 17. The only such divisors are $\boxed{1, -1, 17, -17}$.

Problem 5-3

Method I: Call the height of the tower h. Since $m\angle SQR = 60°$, $\frac{h}{y} = \sqrt{3}$. Since $m\angle SPR = 30°$, $\frac{500+y}{h} = \sqrt{3}$. Multiply these two equations and solve: $y = 250$. Finally, $x = 500+y = \boxed{750}$.

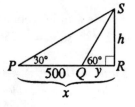

Method II: Since $\triangle PQS$ is isosceles, $QS = 500 = 2QR$, so $y = 250$ and $x = 500+250 = 750$.

Problem 5-4

$$\left(\left(\frac{5}{4}\right)^4\right)^{(5/4)^5} = \left(\left(\frac{5}{4}\right)^4\right)^{\frac{5^5}{4^5}}$$

$$= \left(\frac{5}{4}\right)^{\frac{5^5}{4^4}} = \left(\left(\frac{5}{4}\right)^5\right)^{\frac{5^4}{4^4}} = \left(\left(\frac{5}{4}\right)^5\right)^{\left(\frac{5}{4}\right)^4} = \left(\left(\frac{5}{4}\right)^5\right)^x,$$

so $x = \boxed{\left(\frac{5}{4}\right)^4}$.

Problem 5-5

Let the sum equal S. Then
$$S = 2^{64} + 2^{64} + 2^{48} + 2^{32} + 2^{20} + 2^{12}$$
$$= 2^{12}(2^{52} + 2^{52} + 2^{36} + 2^{20} + 2^8 + 1).$$
Since the number in parentheses on the right is an odd number, the value of k is $\boxed{12}$.

Problem 5-6

Method I: Whenever $a \geq 1$, $\log_b a \leq 1$ if and only if 1) $0 < b < 1$, or 2) $a \leq b$, or 3) $a = 1$. In this problem, since x is real, $x^2+1 \geq 1$. The first condition is satisfied if $0 < 2x+4 < 1 \Leftrightarrow -2 < x < -3/2$. The second condition is satisfied if $x^2+1 \leq 2x+4 \Leftrightarrow x^2-2x-3 \leq 0 \Leftrightarrow (x-3)(x+1) \leq 0 \Leftrightarrow -1 \leq x \leq 3$. The third condition is satisfied if $x^2+1 = 1 \Leftrightarrow x = 0$. Therefore, the original inequality is satisfied by $\boxed{\{x \mid -2 < x < -\frac{3}{2}\} \cup \{x \mid -1 \leq x \leq 3\}}$, which may be written, instead, as a disjunction, using the word *or*.

Method II: By the change of base theorem for logarithms, $\log_b a = \dfrac{\log_c a}{\log_c b}$, (where each base is a positive number different from 1). Therefore, we can write
$$\log_{2x+4}(x^2+1) \leq 1 \Leftrightarrow \frac{\log_{10}(x^2+1)}{\log_{10}(2x+4)} \leq 1, \quad 2x+4 > 0,$$
and $2x+4 \neq 1$. These last two conditions imply that $x > -2$ and $x \neq -3/2$. Now consider the sign of the denominator.

Case I: If $\log_{10}(2x+4) > 0$, then $2x+4 > 1$, so $x > -3/2$. Cross-multiplying and eliminating the logs, $x^2+1 \leq 2x+4$. Solving as in Method I, $-1 \leq x \leq 3$.

Case II: If $\log_{10}(2x+4) < 0$, then $0 < 2x+4 < 1$, so $-2 < x < -3/2$. Cross-multiplying and eliminating logs, $x^2+1 \geq 2x+4$. Solving, $x \leq -1$ or $x \geq 3$. Combining all conditions in Case II, $-2 < x < -3/2$.

Combine Case I and Case II to get the final answer.

Contests written and compiled by Steven R. Conrad & Daniel Flegler   Mathematics Leagues Inc., © 1991

Problem 6-1

Method I: Tricycles and bicycles both have 2 pedals, but tricycles have 3 wheels while bicycles have 2 wheels. Thus, the excess of wheels over pedals must be the number of tricycles, and $176-152 = \boxed{24}$.

Method II: If there are b bicycles and t tricycles, then the total number of wheels is $2b+3t$ and the total number of pedals is $2b+2t$. Since $2b+3t = 176$ and $2b+2t = 152$, $(2b+3t) - (2b+2t) = t = 24$.

Problem 6-2

The original equation is equivalent to $1000x^2 + 1000x = 1000$. Dividing by 1000, $x^2+x = \boxed{1}$.

Problem 6-3

If the length of each leg of the isosceles triangle is $2r$, then the length of the hypotenuse is $2r\sqrt{2}$. The sum of the areas of the three semicircles is $\frac{1}{2}\pi r^2 + \frac{1}{2}\pi r^2 + \frac{1}{2}\pi(r\sqrt{2})^2 = 2\pi r^2$. Hence, $2\pi r^2 = 200\pi$. The area of the isosceles right triangle is $2r^2 = \boxed{200}$.

Problem 6-4

Method I: The left-hand side of the first equation will be rewritten as the difference of two squares, and then we'll factor.

$x^2+xy+y^2 = 84$
$\Leftrightarrow x^2+2xy+y^2 - xy = 84$
$\Leftrightarrow (x+y)^2 - (\sqrt{xy})^2 = 84$
$\Leftrightarrow (x+y + \sqrt{xy})(x+y - \sqrt{xy}) = 84.$

Since we know that $x+y+\sqrt{xy} = 14$, it follows that $x+y-\sqrt{xy} = 6$. Adding and simplifying, $x+y = 10$. Substituting, $\sqrt{xy} = 4$, from which $xy = 16$. Finally, since $x > y$, the only solution is $\boxed{(8,2)}$.

Method II: Completing the square on the first equation, $(x+y)^2 = 84+xy$. Into this, substitute the value of $x+y$ from the second equation, getting $(14-\sqrt{xy})^2 = 84+xy$. Expanding the left side of this equation and simplifying, $\sqrt{xy} = 4$. Substituting this into the second of the original equations and simplifying, we get $x+y = 10$. Since $xy = 16$ and $x > y$, the only solution is $(8,2)$.

Problem 6-5

Since $\tan\theta = \frac{\sin\theta}{\cos\theta}$, and we are given that $\cos\theta = 2\tan\theta$, it follows that $\cos^2\theta = 2\sin\theta$. Solving for $\sin\theta$, we get $\sin\theta = \frac{1}{2}\cos^2\theta$. Since $\sin^2\theta+\cos^2\theta = 1$, we know that $(\frac{1}{2}\cos^2\theta)^2+\cos^2\theta = 1$. Simplifying and clearing fractions, $\cos^4\theta+4\cos^2\theta-4 = 0$. Using the quadratic formula and taking the positive root, we find that $\cos^2\theta = \boxed{-2 + 2\sqrt{2}}$.

Problem 6-6

Brian has a total of $4¢ + 15¢ + 20¢ + 50¢ = 89¢$, so the largest *possible* number of different sums of money he can make is 89. Since he has 4 pennies, he can make $1¢$, $2¢$, $3¢$, and $4¢$. Using one of the nickels and the appropriate number of pennies, he can make any amount from $5¢$ to $9¢$. Using one dime and the appropriate number of pennies, he can make any amount from $10¢$ to $14¢$. Using three nickels and the appropriate number of pennies, he can make any amount from $15¢$ to $19¢$. Using two dimes and the appropriate amount of pennies, he can make any amount from $20¢$ to $24¢$. Thus, Brian can make any amount of money from $1¢$ to $24¢$. Since he has two quarters, he can make all the remaining amounts from $25¢$ to $74¢$. Finally, it is easy to show that every amount from $75¢$ to $89¢$ can be made. Therefore, the total number of different sums of money that Brian can make is $\boxed{89}$.

Contests written and compiled by Steven R. Conrad & Daniel Flegler   Mathematics Leagues Inc., © 1991

Answers &
Difficulty Ratings
November, 1982 – April, 1991

Answers

	1982-1983			**1983-1984**			**1984-1985**
1-1.	100^2 *or* 10 000		1-1.	8 A.M.		1-1.	1984
1-2.	16		1-2.	8%		1-2.	12π
1-3.	909		1-3.	4		1-3.	8
1-4.	4:24		1-4.	60		1-4.	13
1-5.	360		1-5.	$\sqrt{65}$		1-5.	5, 6, 8, 17, 30, 56
1-6.	(2,3), (3,2), $(-1+\sqrt{2},-1-\sqrt{2})$, $(-1-\sqrt{2},-1-\sqrt{2})$		1-6.	(3,3,3), (−4,−4,−4), (1,1,11), (1,11,1), (11,1,1)		1-6.	1
2-1.	−1982		2-1.	9		2-1.	0
2-2.	4		2-2.	60 *or* 60°		2-2.	37 037 037 037
2-3.	10 *or* 10%		2-3.	−2, 4		2-3.	22
2-4.	2		2-4.	*A*		2-4.	260
2-5.	105		2-5.	126		2-5.	(1,6), (11,6)
2-6.	15 *or* 15°		2-6.	52 *or* 52nd *or* "last"		2-6.	150
3-1.	18		3-1.	$\sqrt{50}$ *or* $5\sqrt{2}$		3-1.	1, 2
3-2.	$5,\frac{1}{5}$		3-2.	(16,1), (4,2), (2,4)		3-2.	1985
3-3.	95		3-3.	21		3-3.	28
3-4.	2		3-4.	19		3-4.	12
3-5.	$4\sqrt{3}-2\pi$		3-5.	$\frac{28}{5}$		3-5.	−5
3-6.	−2		3-6.	$-2+\sqrt[3]{-16}$		3-6.	5
4-1.	1, 3, 7		4-1.	17		4-1.	2
4-2.	2, −4		4-2.	16		4-2.	(314,565)
4-3.	9 *or* 9°		4-3.	$\left(-\frac{76}{100},0\right)$ *or* $\left(-\frac{19}{25},0\right)$		4-3.	−1, −6
4-4.	$\frac{3}{5}$		4-4.	0		4-4.	10
4-5.	−6, −10		4-5.	$\frac{49}{25}$		4-5.	$\frac{1}{4},\frac{2}{7}$
4-6.	24		4-6.	392		4-6.	8
5-1.	9		5-1.	16		5-1.	9
5-2.	151		5-2.	12		5-2.	8
5-3.	0		5-3.	3, 4		5-3.	25
5-4.	215 *or* 215°		5-4.	$40 000		5-4.	1
5-5.	−5		5-5.	−1		5-5.	$\frac{\pi}{8},\frac{3\pi}{8},\frac{5\pi}{8},\frac{7\pi}{8}$
5-6.	$\sqrt{3}$		5-6.	30°, 150°, 210°, 330°		5-6.	150
6-1.	28		6-1.	0		6-1.	1
6-2.	625		6-2.	16		6-2.	50
6-3.	3		6-3.	0 *or* 16		6-3.	−1, 0, 1
6-4.	999		6-4.	(3,2)		6-4.	8
6-5.	11		6-5.	5, 6, 7		6-5.	$\frac{1}{3}$
6-6.	$-\frac{1}{2}$		6-6.	121π		6-6.	$(x+1)(x^2+x+1)(x^2-x-1)$

Answers

	1985-1986		**1986-1987**		**1987-1988**
1-1.	16π	1-1.	4	1-1.	-1
1-2.	± 6	1-2.	49	1-2.	6
1-3.	$\left(\frac{101}{2},\frac{99}{2}\right)$	1-3.	-3	1-3.	$-1,1$
1-4.	1	1-4.	677	1-4.	7
1-5.	5	1-5.	0 *or* none	1-5.	$a = -b + 1$
1-6.	4	1-6.	(0,0,0), (2,2,0), (2,0,2), (0,2,2)	1-6.	3
2-1.	1985^2 *or* $3\,940\,225$	2-1.	1	2-1.	8
2-2.	10	2-2.	$\pm 2, \pm 4$	2-2.	(0,0)
2-3.	47	2-3.	0	2-3.	20
2-4.	4000	2-4.	99 days	2-4.	1987
2-5.	*A & 3 or first & last*	2-5.	$144°$	2-5.	16
2-6.	64	2-6.	40	2-6.	659
3-1.	x^3	3-1.	black Dodge	3-1.	0,1
3-2.	6	3-2.	$-1987, 1$	3-2.	32
3-3.	0	3-3.	72	3-3.	$24 + 4\pi$
3-4.	16	3-4.	-2	3-4.	$\frac{2}{3}, 1$
3-5.	$(2x+1)(2x^2+2x+1)$	3-5.	$75°$	3-5.	41.5%
3-6.	-2	3-6.	400	3-6.	21978
4-1.	8	4-1.	64	4-1.	25 *or* 25%
4-2.	$-1, 1$	4-2.	0, 100	4-2.	1988
4-3.	9412	4-3.	16	4-3.	44
4-4.	$\frac{3}{4}$	4-4.	0	4-4.	$45° < x < 135°$
4-5.	$\sqrt{61}$	4-5.	$12\,345\,679$	4-5.	16
4-6.	455	4-6.	18, 23, 28	4-6.	(3,4), (4,3), $(-2+\sqrt{3},-2-\sqrt{3})$, $(-2-\sqrt{3},-2+\sqrt{3})$
5-1.	11	5-1.	130	5-1.	4
5-2.	$10\sqrt{2}$ *or* $\sqrt{200}$	5-2.	a round peg in a square hole	5-2.	-10^5 *or* $-100\,000$
5-3.	$2^{2^{22}}$	5-3.	-2	5-3.	16
5-4.	3973	5-4.	17	5-4.	24
5-5.	(0,0), (0,90), (90,0), (90,90)	5-5.	350	5-5.	80
5-6.	$\frac{60}{11}$	5-6.	352	5-6.	$-\frac{16}{7} < a < -1$
6-1.	1	6-1.	0	6-1.	1987
6-2.	$5\sqrt{2}$	6-2.	8	6-2.	0, 1, 3, 4
6-3.	11	6-3.	$6\frac{1}{2}$	6-3.	$1, \frac{d}{c}, \frac{b+d}{a+c}, \frac{b}{a}, \frac{bd}{ac}$
6-4.	2	6-4.	$\frac{1}{2}$ *or* 50% *or* 0.5	6-4.	$\frac{5}{8}$
6-5.	45 *or* $45°$	6-5.	3:20	6-5.	$\frac{2\pi}{9}$
6-6.	$\frac{2}{3}$	6-6.	$-\frac{1}{4}$	6-6.	$x \geq 2$

Answers

	1988-1989		1989-1990		1990-1991
1-1.	555	1-1.	36	1-1.	$\frac{1990}{1991}$
1-2.	Bob	1-2.	1	1-2.	2000 *or* 2000%
1-3.	1988	1-3.	$\frac{1}{2}$	1-3.	13
1-4.	$\frac{1}{100}$	1-4.	10	1-4.	24
1-5.	5:52 PM	1-5.	$\frac{1}{3}$, 0	1-5.	−1
1-6.	(4,6,2), (−4,−6,−2)	1-6.	2^{1000}	1-6.	43
2-1.	994	2-1.	1	2-1.	0
2-2.	3	2-2.	2	2-2.	199
2-3.	(2,4), (4,2), (16,1)	2-3.	11	2-3.	(0,0), (1,0), (0,1)
2-4.	1	2-4.	13	2-4.	6 *or* 6 km
2-5.	$\frac{9}{4}$	2-5.	1, −3	2-5.	420
2-6.	6, 22	2-6.	60	2-6.	52
3-1.	0	3-1.	2	3-1.	80
3-2.	2	3-2.	100π	3-2.	18
3-3.	$x \le 0$	3-3.	Crocus	3-3.	5
3-4.	i) (1,0) *and* 2 pairs of the form (−1,*b*), with *b* any real number; *or* ii) three pairs of the form: (−1,*b*)	3-4.	(100,1), (10,20)	3-4.	15
3-5.	−5	3-5.	(3,2), $\left(-\frac{2}{5},\frac{3}{5}\right)$	3-5.	128
3-6.	$\frac{13}{2}$	3-6.	$-1 < p < 2$	3-6.	$\frac{4}{7}$
4-1.	(3,3,3)	4-1.	5	4-1.	3
4-2.	Sandy	4-2.	2	4-2.	72 *or* 72°
4-3.	19th	4-3.	15	4-3.	$4\sqrt{2}$
4-4.	0	4-4.	$-19 < x < 19$	4-4.	1990^{1991}
4-5.	32	4-5.	15°, 75°	4-5.	$5\sqrt{2}-4$
4-6.	(5,7)	4-6.	$\frac{663}{662}$	4-6.	−255
5-1.	17, 18, 19	5-1.	(−2,−3), (−3,−2)	5-1.	4
5-2.	10, −10	5-2.	19	5-2.	1, −1, 17, −17
5-3.	13	5-3.	1, 4, 9	5-3.	750
5-4.	12	5-4.	1575	5-4.	$\left(\frac{5}{4}\right)^4$
5-5.	$5\pi + 17$	5-5.	80	5-5.	12
5-6.	1, 48	5-6.	$\frac{1}{6}$	5-6.	$\{x\,|\,-2 < x < -\frac{3}{2}\} \cup \{x\,|\,-1 \le x \le 3\}$
6-1.	1	6-1.	121	6-1.	24
6-2.	5	6-2.	$8\sqrt{2}$	6-2.	1
6-3.	*A*	6-3.	$\frac{1}{3}$	6-3.	200
6-4.	11	6-4.	1990	6-4.	(8,2)
6-5.	$\frac{5}{14}$	6-5.	24	6-5.	$-2+\sqrt{2}$
6-6.	8	6-6.	−16	6-6.	89

Difficulty Ratings

(% correct of 5 highest-scoring students from each participating school)

1982-1983		1983-1984		1984-1985		1985-1986		1986-1987	
1-1.	91%	1-1.	95%	1-1.	87%	1-1.	90%	1-1.	95%
1-2.	96%	1-2.	97%	1-2.	86%	1-2.	92%	1-2.	98%
1-3.	68%	1-3.	93%	1-3.	59%	1-3.	83%	1-3.	69%
1-4.	90%	1-4.	83%	1-4.	87%	1-4.	87%	1-4.	67%
1-5.	64%	1-5.	8%	1-5.	2%	1-5.	71%	1-5.	50%
1-6.	2½%	1-6.	½%	1-6.	35%	1-6.	38%	1-6.	17%
2-1.	90%	2-1.	90%	2-1.	84%	2-1.	90%	2-1.	95%
2-2.	81%	2-2.	48%	2-2.	71%	2-2.	91%	2-2.	77%
2-3.	80%	2-3.	80%	2-3.	18%	2-3.	38%	2-3.	51%
2-4.	62%	2-4.	78%	2-4.	20%	2-4.	78%	2-4.	66%
2-5.	73%	2-5.	79%	2-5.	33%	2-5.	47%	2-5.	71%
2-6.	24%	2-6.	37%	2-6.	1¼%	2-6.	29%	2-6.	18%
3-1.	98%	3-1.	86%	3-1.	92%	3-1.	71%	3-1.	97%
3-2.	91%	3-2.	93%	3-2.	83%	3-2.	72%	3-2.	83%
3-3.	93%	3-3.	72%	3-3.	61%	3-3.	76%	3-3.	86%
3-4.	47%	3-4.	90%	3-4.	56%	3-4.	86%	3-4.	89%
3-5.	33%	3-5.	73%	3-5.	30%	3-5.	40%	3-5.	52%
3-6.	11%	3-6.	1½%	3-6.	7½%	3-6.	1¼%	3-6.	40%
4-1.	93%	4-1.	90%	4-1.	49%	4-1.	90%	4-1.	95%
4-2.	85%	4-2.	75%	4-2.	90%	4-2.	93%	4-2.	94%
4-3.	72%	4-3.	72%	4-3.	47%	4-3.	84%	4-3.	92%
4-4.	40%	4-4.	73%	4-4.	31%	4-4.	61%	4-4.	74%
4-5.	31%	4-5.	23%	4-5.	14%	4-5.	60%	4-5.	81%
4-6.	23%	4-6.	¼%	4-6.	51%	4-6.	12%	4-6.	18%
5-1.	94%	5-1.	82%	5-1.	90%	5-1.	71%	5-1.	92%
5-2.	70%	5-2.	97%	5-2.	82%	5-2.	67%	5-2.	84%
5-3.	68%	5-3.	86%	5-3.	72%	5-3.	36%	5-3.	63%
5-4.	35%	5-4.	71%	5-4.	61%	5-4.	24%	5-4.	37%
5-5.	37%	5-5.	24%	5-5.	5%	5-5.	38%	5-5.	12%
5-6.	2½%	5-6.	2½%	5-6.	26%	5-6.	17%	5-6.	5%
6-1.	84%	6-1.	98%	6-1.	91%	6-1.	93%	6-1.	98%
6-2.	87%	6-2.	87%	6-2.	70%	6-2.	86%	6-2.	76%
6-3.	82%	6-3.	43%	6-3.	71%	6-3.	85%	6-3.	62%
6-4.	52%	6-4.	82%	6-4.	67%	6-4.	90%	6-4.	71%
6-5.	45%	6-5.	22%	6-5.	7%	6-5.	53%	6-5.	66%
6-6.	8½%	6-6.	10%	6-6.	12%	6-6.	21%	6-6.	3%

Difficulty Ratings

(% correct of 5 highest-scoring students from each participating school)

1987-1988		1988-1989		1989-1990		1990-1991	
1-1.	97%	1-1.	95%	1-1.	97%	1-1.	81%
1-2.	95%	1-2.	94%	1-2.	95%	1-2.	72%
1-3.	92%	1-3.	40%	1-3.	55%	1-3.	91%
1-4.	22%	1-4.	67%	1-4.	12%	1-4.	78%
1-5.	30%	1-5.	31%	1-5.	24%	1-5.	20%
1-6.	49%	1-6.	17%	1-6.	10%	1-6.	9%
2-1.	84%	2-1.	91%	2-1.	84%	2-1.	91%
2-2.	72%	2-2.	93%	2-2.	82%	2-2.	97%
2-3.	41%	2-3.	90%	2-3.	63%	2-3.	91%
2-4.	41%	2-4.	83%	2-4.	90%	2-4.	84%
2-5.	66%	2-5.	40%	2-5.	52%	2-5.	83%
2-6.	38%	2-6.	8½%	2-6.	19%	2-6.	42%
3-1.	98%	3-1.	65%	3-1.	80%	3-1.	83%
3-2.	90%	3-2.	90%	3-2.	84%	3-2.	85%
3-3.	61%	3-3.	86%	3-3.	81%	3-3.	51%
3-4.	32%	3-4.	32%	3-4.	87%	3-4.	66%
3-5.	43%	3-5.	11%	3-5.	10%	3-5.	17%
3-6.	17%	3-6.	14%	3-6.	2%	3-6.	7%
4-1.	97%	4-1.	92%	4-1.	96%	4-1.	90%
4-2.	90%	4-2.	74%	4-2.	83%	4-2.	85%
4-3.	83%	4-3.	38%	4-3.	80%	4-3.	52%
4-4.	24%	4-4.	80%	4-4.	74%	4-4.	88%
4-5.	29%	4-5.	53%	4-5.	6%	4-5.	12%
4-6.	1%	4-6.	22%	4-6.	19%	4-6.	7%
5-1.	91%	5-1.	62%	5-1.	75%	5-1.	95%
5-2.	97%	5-2.	80%	5-2.	61%	5-2.	68%
5-3.	86%	5-3.	92%	5-3.	81%	5-3.	62%
5-4.	42%	5-4.	43%	5-4.	90%	5-4.	53%
5-5.	34%	5-5.	21%	5-5.	36%	5-5.	40%
5-6.	3½%	5-6.	4%	5-6.	4%	5-6.	1%
6-1.	92%	6-1.	78%	6-1.	91%	6-1.	91%
6-2.	86%	6-2.	82%	6-2.	72%	6-2.	84%
6-3.	74%	6-3.	80%	6-3.	60%	6-3.	42%
6-4.	33%	6-4.	21%	6-4.	23%	6-4.	73%
6-5.	30%	6-5.	15%	6-5.	69%	6-5.	13%
6-6.	3%	6-6.	48%	6-6.	5%	6-6.	60%

Math League Contest Books
4th Grade Through High School Levels

Written by Steven R. Conrad and Daniel Flegler, recipients of President Reagan's 1985 Presidential Awards for Excellence in Mathematics Teaching, each book provides schools and students with problems from regional interscholastic competitions.

- Contests are designed for a 30-minute period
- Problems range from straightforward to challenging
- Contests from 4th grade through high school
- Easy-to-use format

1-10 copies of any one book: $12.95 each ($16.95 Canadian)
11 or more copies of any one book: $9.95 each ($12.95 Canadian)

Use the form below (or a copy) to order your books

Name _____

Address _____

City _____ State _____ Zip _____
                                 (or Province)   (or Postal Code)

Available Titles	**# of Copies**	**Cost**
Math Contests—Grades 4, 5, 6 (Vol. 1) Contests from 1979-80 through 1985-86	_____	_____
Math Contests—Grades 4, 5, 6 (Vol. 2) Contests from 1986-87 through 1990-91	_____	_____
Math Contests—Grades 7 & 8 (Vol. 1) Contests from 1977-78 through 1981-82	_____	_____
Math Contests—Grades 7 & 8 (Vol. 2) Contests from 1982-83 through 1990-91	_____	_____
Math Contests—High School (Vol. 1) Contests from 1977-78 through 1981-82	_____	_____
Math Contests—High School (Vol. 2) Contests from 1982-83 through 1990-91	_____	_____
Shipping and Handling		$3.00

Please allow 4-6 weeks for delivery   Total: $_____

☐ Check or Purchase Order Enclosed; **or**

☐ Visa / MasterCard # _____

☐ Expiration Date _____ Signature _____

Mail your order with payment to:

Math League Press
P.O. Box 720
Tenafly, NJ 07670

Phone: (201) 568-6328 • Fax: (201) 816-0125